VISIONS
MIT® INTERVIEWS

Andrea Frank

edited by
Jerry Adler

produced at the
MIT Visual Arts Program I SA+P

ACKNOWLEDGEMENTS

I would like to express my deepest gratitude to the following individuals:

- To my MIT Undergraduate Research Opportunity (UROP) students—especially Renee Reder, and also Zach Gazak, Denver Thomas, and Suhni Chung—who enthusiastically collaborated on all aspects of the production of this book. Without them this project would not have been possible.
- To Jan Wampler, who strongly encouraged me to go forward in the beginning stages of this project.
- To Martin Demaine for his test interview and his continuous inspiration.
- To Hiroko Onoda who generously donated her time for interview editing in the beginning stages when there was no funding available.
- To Lori Gross for her valuable and informed feedback and support along the way.
- To Larissa Harris for her inspiring conversations around the project.
- To Susan Cohen and all the wonderful people at the Council for the Arts at MIT for their interest and financial support.
- To Gary van Zante for his help conceptualizing and realizing the project's launch and presentation within MIT.
- To all the wonderful people in the MIT Visual Arts Program and throughout the entire Institute for a fabulous work environment.
- To Jerry Adler for his concise and excellent editing, as well as his invaluable artistic help with conceptual decisions.

Last but not least, I treasure as a true gift the welcoming attitude of, and inspiring interactions with, my conversation partners. They all made this book possible by thoughtfully and generously conveying their fascinating and complex research in layman's terms.

INTRODUCTION

I am deeply interested in and concerned by today's urgent and diverse global challenges. Inspired by the fact that in every hallway at MIT, where I teach Photography and Related Media in the MIT Visual Arts Program, there are world-class minds conducting cutting-edge research, I set out to sew together disparate threads by creating a kaleidoscopic subjective interview collection.

The interviewees for this volume were asked to reflect upon aspects of their research that address current pressing issues such as climate change, geo-political instabilities, adverse effects of globalization, the energy crisis, social tensions, and health epidemics. While some interviewees deal with these challenges directly in their research, others nip at the edges, shadows, and depths in more abstract and conceptual work. The choice and sequencing of the interviews in this compilation encourages the reader to make cross-connections among many disciplines. By recognizing the unifying elements that run throughout, and by joining together starkly different pieces of the same puzzle, the reader will gain a unique apprehension of not just each individual subject, but the entire human curriculum.

Naturally, my choice of interviewees is subjective, and I surely have omitted many strong voices. This is not an exhaustive and complete overview of the work performed at MIT, but rather a sampling of what goes on in this fantastic institution.

For the purpose of consistency, all interviews are structured around four simple questions: the focus of interviewee's work, recent changes in and around the respective field, the global context and visions for the future, and possible implications or downsides.

More information about the interviewees and about MIT can be found online at web.mit.edu.

Andrea Frank
December 2007

CONTENTS

VISIONS
MIT INTERVIEWS

DANIEL NOCERA

Henry Dreyfus Professor of Energy and Professor of Chemistry

What are you working on?

My field is solar energy conversion. We work to convert solar energy into chemical energy. Imagine a world where there is no need for oil. What will replace it? The answer is sunlight plus water. I could almost write an equation, sunlight + water = oil. It's true that a lot of science has to happen before that is possible, but really, what is a fuel? What is oil? It's a compound of high-energy bonds. When you burn the fuel, you get new compounds, the bonds have less energy in them, and the energy that is released is the power that you use. So, when you burn oil or gasoline in a car, the chemical bonds of the gasoline rearrange with oxygen inside the piston to make CO_2 and water, and from this rearrangement you get energy.

Let me explain what I mean when I say sunlight + water = oil. In order to create energy from water, you must split the hydrogen and oxygen molecules. You've got to rearrange the bonds. Now, if you just shine sunlight on water nothing happens. So what's my research? My research is to make the thing in between, the thing that catches the sunlight and then acts on the water to rearrange its low-energy bonds into high-energy bonds of hydrogen and oxygen. Oil already has the high-energy bonds, put there millions of years ago by the compression of fossils and plant matter. It's essentially stored solar energy. The bonds of water are low-energy. Therefore we must use sunlight to rearrange them into high-energy H_2 and O_2 bonds. Once that is done, we can—exactly as we do with oil—rearrange them again to create low-energy bonds of water, and the excess energy is what you use. Bond rearrangement is the essence of the energy problem. It is going to be the science that delivers the gift of the sun as our power source.

How will you accomplish this?

We use nature as our blueprint. A leaf is a solar energy machine. It uses light to make oxygen and hydrogen. People don't know that, but it's a solid form of hydrogen (NADH) that gets stored with CO_2 to make sugar. So, we try to figure out how a leaf works. We do this by capturing its essential ingredients and making compounds that have its basic elements. Our task is to replace the leaf with a substance that can effectively do the same job. That's called artificial photosynthesis. We literally build molecules that can capture

light and then act on water to perform this hydrogen and oxygen splitting. After making the compounds bond by bond, we expose them to lasers in order to imitate the effects of the sun. The lasers allow us to turn the light on and off quickly and observe what happens to all that energy. The light produces an excited state. We can then take a series of pictures and follow molecules and energy flow. When we see how energy is captured in the excited state, we try to convey it to the water molecule. If we see that things aren't working well we go back. It's like being an engineer of molecules. We change the molecules around, we add things, we take things away, and, hopefully, we make a better molecule.

What has happened in the recent past that has affected your field?

This is really simple. I'm the solar energy guy. I've been worrying about this solar energy problem since I started my career in 1979. Not many people listened. All of a sudden, if you look in any newspaper, you see articles about solar energy. If I talk to anybody on the street, it's energy, energy, energy. So why do you think that happened? I'll let you answer it.

Because greater numbers of people need greater quantities of energy than ever before and the byproducts of that energy usage are ruining our environment.

That's what a lot of people would say. But to be perfectly honest, we don't care about the environment. The human race has never cared about the environment. For a small part of our population—for people who are thoughtful, concerned, caring, and nurturing—the state of the environment is a true cause for concern. What most people are concerned about is Gross Domestic Product. GDP scales linearly with energy use. The more energy you use, the richer you are.

Think about the way you live and everything you use. You're benefiting from a really good economy. That means you're using a lot of energy. I have all the numbers for world energy use per person in whatever country you want to know about. We're all at fault for this. It is wrong to say that there are some callous or ignorant people who only worry about economics and making money and therefore they are the ones responsible for this. That is not true. We're all to blame. We all take part in the actions that have created this problem, it's just that there are some of us who are also worried about the consequences of those actions.

Why is Kyoto failing? It's not because people don't want to conserve. It's because Kyoto was treated as an environmental issue. It's not. It's an economic issue. Economy is tied to energy use, and energy use is tied to CO_2 production. Countries that didn't sign on to it said they didn't want to change their economy. Other countries said they recognized the urgency of this environmental issue and said they would change their economy. Well guess what, not one country has changed its economy. People who are meeting the Kyoto accord have just restructured things to make it look like they have. The fact that no country has actually changed its economy reflects the fact that nobody really cares about the environment. It's not a big enough driver. You'd think it should be, but it really isn't.

One way to disconnect this chain of GDP, energy use, and environmental pollution is to get rid of carbon. If you can break that dependence, if you can snip that connection, then you can grow economies and be environmentally sound at the same time. That's why my research is so important. I'm snipping that connection between economic growth, energy use, and CO_2.

It's appropriate that we are doing this interview today, September 12, 2006. It would have been even more appropriate yesterday because September 11th was a big eye opener for this country and the world. We figured out that there are a lot of geo-political consequences to relying on oil and getting it out of the Middle East. Of course, they've always been there. We've always known about it. But the issue hasn't been as prevalent because, as you said, there weren't as many people needing the energy. As that demand increases, this geo-political instability becomes more obvious. September 11th was like a two by four over our heads. And when I say ours, I mean the global community, not just the Americans. As a global community, we awakened to the fact that if we're going to need a lot of energy and we're going to rely on the Middle East, it's probably going to lead to a lot of geo-political unrest. This issue is what we call energy security.

The other big driver is cost. Higher demand means higher prices. The environment has always been an issue, but security and cost are the two new players. It's all happened in the last five years and it's totally changed my research program because I don't need to justify what I do anymore. People understand the importance now. Even in 1995, even at MIT, people said, "Now Nocera, why are you trying to run your reactions with light? Why don't you just heat it?" In other words, why do you spend all this time worrying about light when you can just turn on the heat? So it's not just the regular people, even my colleagues at MIT couldn't get it. That tells you how deep the problem is. We're doing terrible things. I can give you statistics. I'm a walking encyclopedia of this stuff. It's very scary.

Will you put it into a nutshell?

This is the nutshell. Right now, whether you realize it or not, you are living in an experiment that we don't know the consequences of. We can drill cores in the ice, examine the trapped bubbles, and determine the CO_2 concentration for times past. It's totally simple. We can go back 650,000 years and see that CO_2 levels were never over 310 parts per million. I always say that if CO_2 were colored purple, we would all be scared shitless. If in 1900 it would have been just a purple haze, now we wouldn't see through the purple, okay? Right now we're at 380. We're headed to 550 to 750 by the end of the century. We better hope those plants keep living, because if they die, this population dies.

Now, here's an interesting thing. When people talk about global climate control, they talk about the earth. I hate that. That is the arrogance of the human race. Do you want to know something? Don't worry about the earth being okay. The earth is fine. Kurt Vonnegut gave a great PBS show a year ago. The way he talked about it was that the earth has its own immune system and if we become really irritable to it, it will just get rid of us. So for all those people that are worried about the health of the earth, don't bother. You'd better just worry about yourself because human beings may become extinct, not the earth.

We are the most vulnerable because we are highest on the food chain. We should be really concerned. The people who aren't, the people who say don't worry about it, for them there is usually another motivating factor, namely money. Just remember, they are the biggest gamblers in the world. If I'm wrong, we'll keep living. But if they're wrong, we're dead. I'm not the gambler. I'm the conservative in this argument.

Where do you see your work in a global context? Where do you see it going?

The global part is totally simple. This is why I get up in the morning. It drags me out every single day. We must break the connection between energy use, the economy, CO_2 emissions, and oil. The result will be a safer, healthier, more environmentally sound, more prosperous world.

Because energy use is tied to economies of scale, the poorest people have the least access to energy. If we can deliver an energy source that will be available to everybody, that's the greatest thing that can be done to eliminate poverty. So, the global consequences of my work are obvious. I'd like to get rid of this precious commodity that only a few people have and which can be accessed only by a very large country with a very large army. This resource can be replaced with the sun, which shines everywhere and on everybody.

And we wouldn't need nuclear energy, for example?

I'd have to say, in the large scale of things, because the energy needs are going to be so great, that the solution won't be any one thing. I do believe that solar energy should be primary, but it's going to be an energy mix. Nuclear isn't that bad if you do it right, but we don't do it right. You need to make fuels that can be re-enriched and that people can't use for weapons proliferation. There needs to be a lot of new science done, and at MIT we do that. We have a great nuclear department.

Would you live next to a nuclear reactor?

Yes, I would have no problems living next to one, absolutely none. Because of the way these reactors work now, they are almost totally safe. Why wouldn't you want to live next to one, as long as they're not big and ugly? A whole MIT team works on this. These things would be modular. They would look no bigger than your corner store, like a nice looking house. And so, again, it's the power of science and research. You can take something that's scary and bad and make it safe and good. The French are doing the experiment. We don't have any CO_2 being produced in France. They flat lined CO_2 omission because they are using nuclear. If you're really concerned about the environment, which I am, I think you have to look at nuclear.

What are the downsides of your research?

Right now, the biggest downside to solar power is that people are still not committed to it. Everybody has to get on board. It's going to require a community of scientists, a community of politicians, a community of engineers, a community of policy makers, a community of economists, and a community of sociologists. We don't have that yet. We just have a bunch of frontier scientists.

And your students?

Those students are the greatest product I have right now. Every single year I'm churning out kids who are totally passionate about this. I believe that in ten or fifteen years, we can solve it.

Interviewed 9/12/06

ERIC S. LANDER

Professor of Biology, MIT; Professor of Systems Biology, Harvard
Founding Director of Broad Institute of MIT and Harvard

What are you working on?

We're working on understanding the information in the human genome and we're figuring out how to apply that information to medicine. We have an amazing trove that has been piling up for three and a half billion years, and it contains so much information about things like the cellular basis of cancer, the genetic risks for diabetes, the history of the human population, human similarities and differences, mechanisms of evolution, and the way genes behave. The genome is a text that our generation is first to have read. And it's not just a generic human text. We have texts from each individual. We also have text from chimpanzees, dogs, mice, and fish—to name a few.

In some sense, almost all of the potential solutions to medical problems come down to comparing two versions of the text. So much can be learned from the evolutionary processes that gave rise to these texts. We can look at the process of speciation, because different parts of the genome experience different histories. We can look at mechanisms of mutation by comparing human to chimp. We can look at the genetic differences that cause diabetes or Alzheimer's by studying collections of patients with the disease and without. We can discover the genetic causes of cancer by comparing the version of the text in a lung tumor versus in normal tissue. We can study the action of drugs by comparing the differences between lung tumors that respond to a drug and those that don't. If you choose your comparison sensibly, and you ask what aspects of the text are the same in one group and different in another, you can learn a tremendous amount about mechanisms, and a lot about disease.

What we've got, for the first time, is a generic approach to asking questions. In the past in biology, you had to know so much in advance about a topic in order to ask relevant questions. Now, in a sense, you don't have to know so much. You can ask hundreds or thousands of questions. It means that the barrier to investigate any aspect of human medicine has become lower. Now, MIT graduate students, or undergraduates, are able to investigate these questions. In that sense, this technology is throwing the doors open for a generation to take on problems more effectively.

You're saying a student is able to do this. How does it work?

It depends on what you are trying to address. If you want to ask a well-focused question, it's not very hard to do. You could do it in an afternoon. All the data are available on the web. When I say an MIT student can do it, I mean that a student anywhere in the world can do it. Anybody can download the data and work on it, and that is very much part of our principle. We are going to serve patients best by getting the information into the hands of as many people as possible. There should be no barriers. This is a position we feel very strongly about.

The problem is no longer getting access to the data. The problem is how to extract the signal from the noise. It almost always comes down to writing a computer program. The human genome is three billion letters long. That is a lot of information. It is more than you could read if you sat down and tried to do it. You've got to have some idea of what you're looking for. In the human genome, we might ask how many positions of that three billion-letter sequence are commonly variable in the population. By commonly variable, we mean that at least 1% of the population has a different form. We now know the answer is about 12 million sites of variation in the human population. We want to study them in disease. A study of all 12 million in every possible patient is still a lot of work. So we might ask, do we need to know all of them? And it turns out that nearby ones are very well correlated, so indeed we don't need all of them. Maybe we only need a few hundred thousand of them. And as it turns out, we can now make tools to study just those three hundred thousand pretty effectively. You can then use them to find the genetic risk factors for many common diseases.

Is it meaningful that a particular spelling difference is 10% more common in patients with bipolar disease, or is it a statistical fluctuation or perhaps an artifact due to population substructure? Or is it a reflection of the fact that people with bipolar disease might come, say, more from one ethnic group, and the data might show some sort of accidental correlation? Figuring out whether differences really mean something involves both computational biology and laboratory biology.

We're the first generation to read these texts, and I'm sure that all the methods being used are going to be viewed as amateurish by the students that come along ten and twenty years from now. I use the analogy of literature. If you're the first to read Shakespeare, the chance that you're going to extract most of the meaning out of that text is nil. Don't even imagine that. As a beginner, you try to get the plot, or a couple of interesting metaphors.

Well, we're learning how to read this literature, and though it is amazing how rapidly it is going, I'm mindful about how much we are probably missing. But that's okay.

How do we get these letters? Where do you start?

It turns out to be easier than you might think. We spent fifteen years in the human genome project working out methods for genome sequencing with the hope that we wouldn't just end up with one volume on the shelf, but would really have a methodology that would let us investigate any organism. And, that is exactly what has happened. The human genome project probably cost two or three billion dollars over fifteen years, but to do it again right now would cost less than 1% of that. So that is tremendous progress. Getting the basic catalog of human genetic variation probably cost a couple hundred million dollars. But now that we have that information, getting the variation from any one patient costs one thousand dollars. That is amazing, and given another decade it'll probably cost ten or twenty dollars. At the beginning of such projects, some folks worry that it is so expensive. And, if it were going to stay so expensive, it's true that it would be unacceptable. But, as an investment in a learning curve, to eventually be able to get it from any patient for ten bucks, it's quite acceptable. This is a good use for our research dollars. In the United States, our federal research budget for biomedical research is twenty-eight billion dollars a year. The idea that we invested in the neighborhood of 1% of that every year for fifteen years and got to this point strikes me as a great investment.

Have there been any considerable changes in your field in the recent past that have affected your research?

Yes, the field has undergone remarkable technological transformation in the last fifteen years or so. The prospect of sequencing the human genome was madness in 1986 when it was first proposed. It was an attractive goal, but there was just no practical way to do it. It would have taken many hundreds of years to accomplish a project like that.

Where have the advancements been specifically?

It is everything. It is biochemistry, which allows us to prepare and sequence DNA; it is machines to detect DNA; it is computation; and it is human organization, bringing together a type of teamwork that we didn't have in laboratory biology. It is all of those pieces coming together. It is DNA chips with thousands of spots on them where you can squirt on a sample of DNA or RNA. It is a zillion technologies. When I look back to when I started in biology in the early 1980's and compare it to where we are today, it is analogous to early man going out to explore the world on foot, versus having 747's that fly around the globe. It is that level of difference that has happened in two decades. Our ability to explore the genetic world has gone from being the hunter-gatherer of genes—where someone would go off into the bush searching for a gene and might come back with one a year or two later, or perhaps would never be heard from again—to a world where we have complete satellite imagery of the entire genetic globe. The evolution of this worldview, the view that links with ease the local picture and the global picture, is what has happened. I think a lot in terms of images. Nobody can think about the earth without the image of the earth from space, without the images from maps, without knowing that if I travel east I end up in the Atlantic Ocean and if I travel west I get to California. But there was a time when people didn't have that view of the world. That is the kind of change we've gone through in biology, and it is really interesting. We haven't even begun to digest what it means to have our scientific worldview shift so much.

What role do you think your work is playing in a global context? Also, where do you see it going in the long term, say, the next one or two hundred years?

It is tough to predict things a hundred or two hundred years out. In January of 1900, scientists were just rediscovering the laws of genetics. At that time, they didn't have the context and vocabulary to think that in one hundred years we'd have the sequence of the human genome. They didn't even know that there was such a thing as a human genome. So, to predict what will happen in the next hundred years is guaranteed to be foolish.

Things will change so radically. But what effect does it have? The big effect I see is that it really is a generic, systematic, uniform approach to so many problems. Therefore, it is a force of unification in science. The most powerful changes science undergoes are unifications—that is, when people realize that the many different things they are working on all can be viewed from a common perspective. Genomics is providing that common perspective. It is saying that every cell stores and reads out information, and that information can be recorded. I don't want to pretend that it is the solution to all questions. It's not. But it is a common set of terms for discussion for all questions. It is a framework to discuss problems of immunology, of bacteriology, of cardiovascular disease, of cancer. It is also a source for democratization, because smart, young individuals are now able to tackle problems that used to require massive laboratories. Therefore, because of this technology, we are able to address many more problems than ever before.

Where does it all go? Well, we clearly will have a total knowledge of all human genetic variation. I would be surprised if we didn't have a fairly complete correlation of human genetic variation with regard to risk of disease. I think we'll have a very deep knowledge of evolution and the forces that shape the evolution of species. And I think we'll have a deep knowledge of developmental biology. It is very hard to describe, but it is a world in which the terms of discussion are complete. It is a biological world with a kind of 'periodic table'. There was chemistry before the periodic table, but it was unruly and unbounded. And then there was chemistry with the periodic table, where everything was explained in terms of a fixed list of elements. It didn't take away the mystery. It didn't solve all problems. But the world of chemistry was totally different because of that turning point. That is akin to what we are living through now in biology. It's not just the sequence of the genome; it is the entire breadth of what is going on in these couple of decades.

I'm interested in the evolutionary side.

It is very interesting. The evolutionary forces shaping the human genome now are the same as have been shaping mammals for the last hundred million years. As sophisticated as we think we are, what the genome is most interested in is reproduction and fighting off infection. Those are the biggies from the standpoint of evolution. The genes in these processes are the ones that have been evolving most rapidly.

The diversity of life is just stunning. If we look at how many solutions life comes up with, how incredibly creative life is, it is astounding because, in some sense, we are working with a limited set of tools. In the last hundred million years, no really novel genes have been invented in mammals. It's almost all been reuse of old genes. But you can take old parts and make amazing new things out of them. Evolution is extremely conservative, and yet very creative. What that means is that the tools it works with are very evolvable. And I think the most exciting thing would be to deeply understand this ability to evolve.

What are the implications of your work? Is there a downside?

There are many implications. Knowledge itself is neutral. But, what one does with knowledge is not. Understanding that there are, say, seven types of lung cancer, putting them into their own categories, and understanding their molecular mechanism could allow for the development of therapeutics for each different type. That is a compelling mission and it is one of the reasons why we do this type of science. In fact, I think it would be unethical not to do this kind of science. But you could use this knowledge to develop therapeutics that are only available to very rich people. You could use the knowledge of who is predisposed to lung cancer to deny insurance to people. You could use the knowledge of who might be predisposed to manic depression to attack a political candidate. You could invade people's privacy. The question is, whose information is it? And how should the information be used?

Getting to the root of disease is such powerful information. To solve disease, we have to understand the mechanism of disease. Otherwise, we're shooting in the dark. Occasionally we can come up with therapies without understanding the mechanism, but we can't count on that. So, we've got to know what is wrong at the cellular and molecular level. But, in the process of understanding the mechanism, which is the essential tool for making therapeutics, we have to pass through this very uncomfortable phase of being able to describe what is wrong, and even being able to predict what might go wrong, without actually being able to do anything about it.

As far as the misuse of information is concerned, we talk a great deal about this. There might be misuse with respect to employment, insurance, or inequity of access to information for therapeutics. In our work, we try to ensure in as many ways as possible that there are proper safeguards in place to protect the dissemination of this information. For instance, we have been down to Congress to push for legislation for privacy. It would be naïve to think that there will be no misuse. I think the only solution is to continue to press very hard to make sure the good uses happen as rapidly as possible and the misuses, at least, get pointed out as vocally as possible. You hope that if you do that, you'll end up proud of where this all shakes out at the end. I'm mindful that there is nothing truly powerful that does not also have the potential risk of negative consequences. But I would have a hard time explaining to my kids that we didn't pursue this information because we were paralyzed by that possibility.

Can you talk about the difference between the predisposition for a disease and the probability of actually getting it? Also, what are the benefits of this advance knowledge?

Knowing that you have a predisposition may help you a great deal. Take the case of a hemophiliac. A person who knows he has a serious risk of bleeding to death from a clot will change his lifestyle. One can use that information powerfully. On the other hand, knowing that you are at risk for Alzheimer's disease, since there is nothing you can do about it today, might be devastating. In that case, what am I going to gain from knowing? Medical predispositions really should be sorted into the categories of those which can be acted on, and those which cannot.

In either case, people should not leap from the knowledge that they have a particular predisposition to the conclusion that they are going to contract a disease. Sometimes a predisposition might mean a probability increase from 1% to 10%. In that instance, even those who are more inclined toward that specific ailment still most likely won't develop it. On the other hand, for example, with early onset breast cancer, there is a gene that will increase a woman's risk to more than 50%. Certainly, a person with this gene should start mammograms at an earlier age. She'd be crazy not to, because we can do something about breast cancer. This doesn't mean that this person will get breast cancer, but a 50% risk is a significant number that should be taken seriously.

The problem we get into is that there may be a thousand things to know, and understanding each one requires knowledge of a different set of details. So, how do you hand someone a list and say, please check which of the thousand you'd like to know about and we'll lay out for you the consequences of knowing each of those things? Many people feel they should be made aware of all possible options, but often that can be more confusing than it is helpful. Maybe people would be better served by having a health plan that organizes these things into a couple of categories and then provides the option of discovering more in a specific area if one so desires. But right now, and maybe for the next decade, or five decades, we have a bit of a chasm between the predictions and the therapies, and this poses very difficult challenges.

So, we have this murky crystal ball. It doesn't tell us anything with certainty. As scientists, we're not looking at this crystal ball to make predictions about the medical future of individual people. We're looking because of what it is telling us about the genes that cause diseases. We want to understand genes, not to make predictions about specific people, but to make therapies, because the therapies can help anybody.

Interviewed 4/19/06

K. DARON ACEMOGLU

Charles P. Kindleberger Professor of Applied Economics

What are you working on here at MIT?

I'm in the Economics Department here at MIT. Outside of my teaching responsibilities, most of my time is spent on economic growth research. That means understanding how and why societies grow, the consequences of that growth and, perhaps most importantly, why it is that some countries are able to achieve economic growth and better standards of living for their populations while others are not.

Economists have been thinking about these kinds of issues for a long time. Often though, the thinking occurs within old frameworks, and so part of my research is motivated by the consideration of whether we are asking and answering the right questions. The current economics framework has been very good at identifying sources of economic growth in terms of educational achievements, or technology, or organization of markets, but hasn't really dug deeper into why markets are organized differently. Why is it that in some places there is investment into education, or adoption and embracing of new technologies, and in other places there is not? That is basically what brought me to my recent research on political economy and institutions. The major theme that has been keeping me busy right now, and over the past five years at least, is understanding the roles of institutions, how institutions emerge, and why dysfunctional institutions arise in different places.

How do we know that institutions really matter? This sounds like a simple question, but in terms of statistical or econometric structure it is actually rather complicated. A very common view in both policy and academic circles is that to understand the problems of economic development in much of the world—especially places like southern Asia, the Caribbean, and sub-Saharan Africa—one must look at geographic factors. For instance, is the geography and ecology of Africa simply not conducive to development because of hot temperatures and greater soil depletion? In this line of reasoning, we are essentially talking about factors that are outside of human control. And if you look at the approach that many people—the UN, the World Bank, and many economists—take to achieve solutions, it is all about how we can provide aid or intervene in a way that softens the impact of these various inherent disadvantages.

My research is about arguing the opposite of this. The sources of problems in the world are not geographic or predetermined. They are engendered by the institutional organizations within these societies. Now, it is not useless for the World Bank or the International Monetary Fund to funnel aid to educational systems or infrastructure, but it is certainly not a magic bullet. The societies themselves need to be empowered to change their organizations and institutions.

For example, if this diagnosis is correct, the last thing you would want to do is pour aid into a country that is being run by a dictator. That money will just end up in that person's pocket and actually enable him—there are no female dictators as far as I know—to solidify his position in the society. It happened with Mobutu in Zaire during the Cold War. It was very convenient for Mobutu to play the Russians against the Americans and get a lot of financial support while he was pursuing policies that impoverished the rest of his country.

The World Bank and the UN have learned from many past mistakes, but in many ways they are perpetuating the same old behavior. A true solution to the underlying problems really has to be addressed within the internal dynamics of the society. The society itself must to be empowered. This doesn't mean that we in the West, who live in great comfort, should do nothing. There are many things that can be done. Certainly, preventing the most egregious violations of human rights is absolutely essential. The U.S. and Europe could have prevented at least part of the genocide in Rwanda, they could have done any number of things in Darfur, they could now do a lot of things in Chad, and they could have done a lot of things in Liberia in the last days of Charles Taylor. Those are the kinds of things the international community should be much more focused on, rather than trying to run the economies of these countries.

What kinds of institutions are you focusing on?

I think the most important types of institutions are political and economic. Is the society democratic or dictatorial? If it is democratic, what type of procedures of collective decision making are there? For example, how powerful is the executive? Are there checks and balances, such as an independent judiciary? Essentially, is power distributed fairly and proportionally among the branches? Economically, the most important issues surround property development and the enforcement of property rights. Secondary issues would involve the writing of business contracts, loans, checks, and things of that nature.

This is not to deny the importance of social institutions and how people interact. For example, you cannot understand a country like India without understanding the caste system, but I focus on political and economic institutions.

Do you make recommendations to the international community?

It has never been my intention to make strong policy recommendations. The phenomena we are dealing with are incredibly complex, and one of the mistakes that we have made in the social sciences community is making strong recommendations before we truly understand the dimensions of a problem. In such complex relationships, there are many reasons why things are the way they are. It is very easy to see something that looks dysfunctional from the outside, intervene, and then have something more dysfunctional replace it.

Have there been any changes in the recent past that have affected your research?

Economics is still a young discipline, so it is constantly affected by change from within and without. The research on institutions that I've been doing for almost ten years now would not have been accepted as part of mainstream economics in the past. Now it is. And it is very different from similar work that political scientists and sociologists do. It is more quantitatively and theoretically based. I suppose there has been a move in the whole profession toward being more open.

Another aspect of my work has been motivated by events that have led to globalization and increasing inequality among peoples. The premium that more educated workers receive relative to less educated workers has increased not only in the United States, but also in other countries as well. Furthermore, the economic relationships that we have been familiar with were much more relevant and useful in the context of closed economies. This thinking needs to be modified for a world where information flows and people move more fluidly than was the case twenty years ago.

What role do you think your work is playing in a global context and where do you see it going in the future?

This question touches on the topics we talked about earlier. Both to my discomfort and pleasure, I see my work receiving much more attention from international organizations such as the World Bank, the United Nations, and the International Monetary Fund. But it is inevitable that any academic work will not be implemented in its pure academic form when it goes into the field. The people who implement it must create their own synthesis. Sometimes it has nothing to do with the original intentions of the work, and that is a bit scary. Sometimes the World Bank publications talk about institutions and some of the research that I do, and I can't quite recognize it. But I think ultimately, slowly, it will start having an effect, and I hope that my understanding of how things work improves so I can contribute to this process.

What are the implications of your work? Are there downsides?

Yes, I think there are. All human relations are complex, and they become much more complex when we think of them in the context of the socio-political arena. We really don't know the implications of trying new things. Essentially, this work is all about changing institutions. But when that happens, there is always the danger that you are altering something that has evolved for very good reasons.

Take Iraq, for example. People said that the system in Iraq was not good, they had a dictator that they couldn't get rid of, and the solution was to go in and design a democracy for them. So we threw away the old system to replace it with something we thought was better. But a country that has evolved over hundreds of years has evolved that way for a reason, and when you topple old systems because of an ideal of something better, you are actually promoting chaos. We must constantly be aware of this danger.

Take Peru. There is a tremendous amount of corruption in that country. So, logically, the first thing you would want to do is get rid of it. But if you don't change anything else, what you will end up with will be much worse, because corruption is what greases the wheels in Peru. The government regulations there are so bad that without corruption it would be exponentially more difficult to get anything done. You cannot just address one component part of a system. You must address the whole.

This is why I said at the beginning that I feel quite wary about taking some of these lessons to practice before we are really sure about the details. On the other hand, there are real, very dire conditions in the world. People are starving, people are not being educated, a lot of growth potential is being wasted, and a lot of well meaning people want to do something about it—be it aid, be it changing the political system, be it changing the economic institutions. So you try to do something based on whatever ideas appear most promising. But the ideas haven't been tried, and that is the danger.

Interviewed 3/21/06

EDWARD FARHI

Professor of Physics
Director of the Center for Theoretical Physics

What are you working on here at MIT?

The main thing I work on at MIT is the theory of elementary particles, which is an attempt to get a mathematical description of the smallest constituents of matter. We're trying to understand nature at distance scales that are infinitesimal. Now, a lot of people have trouble understanding why we would want to do that. Interestingly, those same people don't seem to have much trouble understanding why someone would want to study the sky. If you ask most people if they think it is worthwhile to study the heavens, they say, "Yes. It's interesting to know what makes stars burn, it's interesting to know what galaxies are made of, it's interesting to know what the universe looked like after the big bang, and it's interesting to know how big the universe is." Well, elementary particle physics is an investigation of nature, but instead of looking out, we look in. We try to understand things on the smallest scales. And it turns out that when you start to look at things on a very, very tiny scale, you start to see phenomena you never would have anticipated.

How would you describe it more specifically?

Let me first briefly describe the theory of elementary particles. There are things called atoms. Atoms have nuclei in the center and electrons going around. Inside the nucleus you have neutrons and protons. Inside neutrons and protons there are particles called quarks. There are six types of quarks in nature. They are alike in some ways and different in others, but everything in nature is made of these six types of quarks. People are made of up quarks and down quarks. Most of the material world is made of up and down quarks. Then there are other quarks we are less familiar with, like the top quark, charm quark, bottom quark, and strange quark.

Where do we find those?

You have to make those in accelerators. But to a particle physicist, the fact that they have to be made, and we're not made of them, doesn't make them any less interesting. They have very similar properties to the particles we're made of. The particles we're made of share the virtue that they're very long lived. If they weren't long lived, they wouldn't be good building blocks. Aside from that distinguishing fact, the other particles we're

interested in have very similar properties.

Let me give you another example. We're also made of electrons. All your atoms have electrons. The electron is a stable particle. It doesn't decay into anything, which, again, is why it is a good building block. You don't make things out of materials that decay. But the electron has a cousin, called the muon, which is exactly like the electron in all respects except that it is heavier than an electron and it can decay into an electron. So the muon is as fundamental as the electron. We're interested in understanding the forces between these particles. How do you describe the interactions between them? Why do they come in these specific varieties? Why do they have the properties they have? These questions are fundamental in terms of our understanding of physics. As a result, society spends a lot of money trying to answer them. There are giant accelerators which have been built to collide particles at extremely high energies in an attempt to understand only this. The real and direct technological spin-offs are not yet evident.

So you wouldn't know where this might be going in terms of useful applications?

Although there have been exceptions, direct technological application of elementary particle physics will have its time in the future. For example, the Large Hadron Collider is the new accelerator that is being built at CERN. CERN is the European Organization for Nuclear Research. These are probably the most complicated experiments ever done by anybody. They require hundreds of scientists to build the devices, and the devices cost billions of dollars to make. This is primarily a laboratory, but along the way, the people there do think of things that help people. The World Wide Web, for example, was invented at CERN as a way for computers to communicate.

As part of research in your field?

Yes. There was a need for computers to communicate better, so they made the World Wide Web and the world benefited. Particle physicists didn't go there with the intention of building the World Wide Web. It just happened. There are other examples, but that's not really what this is about. What it's really about is trying to understand nature at its most fundamental level. That is the quest, and it has been very productive in terms of what it has given the world. There is no real alternative to science when it comes to understanding the world. Science is what makes life miraculous.

What types of changes in the recent past, in and around your field, have affected your research today?

That's interesting. Particle physics has seen major changes in the last twenty to thirty years. There has been a great movement toward abstract mathematics, the development of String Theory, and a real push toward rather grand attempts to understand nature. Many of these attempts became overly mathematical and a bit removed from reality for my taste. Therefore, my area of interest shifted to quantum computation, which is an area of physics where we try to use the known laws of quantum mechanics to increase computer speed. I've worked on that quite a lot and the reasons are twofold. Firstly, I find it interesting. Secondly, I became turned off by the slow progress in standard particle physics.

How is a quantum computer different from what we have today?

If we are ever able to build a quantum computer, it would do things ordinary computers could never do.

When do you think that might happen?

Probably not in the near future. I don't think a functioning quantum computer will exist for quite awhile.

And what would it be able to do exactly?

For one thing, it could factor large numbers very quickly. Now that sounds like an esoteric mathematical application, but if you could factor large numbers that quickly, you could break all banking and military codes. For that reason alone, this field generates significant financial support.

So once that is ready, there will have to be a lot of adjustments.

If a quantum computer were built, there would have to be tremendous adjustments in how people encode information. There's big interest in figuring out if a quantum computer can be built. I really don't work so much on the actual building. I focus on the question of what could be done if it existed. I try to program a nonexistent machine to see if it could do something that an ordinary computer couldn't do.

This is one of the great things about MIT. You get to work on what you like. At some point you have to have results, but there is great freedom to pursue your interests. I'm very grateful to MIT, and when you consider the people who are here, the financial support, and the freedom I've mentioned, it's a perfect place for someone like me to pursue his life's work.

How do you envision your role in a global context and where do you see your work going in the future?

I'm a purist when it comes to science. The virtues are inherent. Science enriches us, and understanding how the world works makes it more, not less, interesting. My mission is my work. First of all, I don't think I'd be good at anything else. Doing something and having people see it is how I think I am capable of affecting the world. Physics and quantum computing are worldwide efforts. For example, just the other day I saw a paper from somebody in Uruguay who is working on something I worked on. That made me happy. It makes me feel good that there are people in faraway countries who read my papers and comment on them. We post papers on the Web and they are instantly read and responded to by people all over the world. But I don't have any real sense of having a mission beyond doing my work, hoping that it is right, of good quality, and accessible to people who are interested in reading it.

Physics is global by definition because anybody can do it. It is entirely democratic and is a pure meritocracy. It's extremely tolerant and open to new ideas from any type of person. If your work is good, you'll be recognized. If you write papers that have results, you'll get ahead. Physics is a lot like professional sports. It doesn't matter who you are. If you score goals in soccer, you play on the best teams. Even if you're a jerk, you still play on the best teams. Physics is the same way. You can be from any culture, any race, either gender, and of any age. As long as your papers are good, it doesn't matter. People don't appreciate that enough. It's very fair. Ultimately, when it comes down to things of lasting value, that's what matters.

What are the possible implications of the implementation of your work? Do you see a downside?

In particle physics, when you talk about implementation, you're talking about something very abstract. It's hard to see how a giant accelerator, like the one at CERN, which is pumping tremendous amounts of energy to circulate particles around a thirty-mile tube and smashing them together to make explosions is going to have direct technological spin-offs. I don't think it should be viewed in that way. It has to be viewed as esoteric research which is enriching us. This is beyond nuclear. These are much higher energy levels per particle. In a nuclear explosion, a lot of energy is released, but there are a lot of particles in that explosion. At CERN, you are dealing with a lot of energy per particle. The energy per particle in an accelerator is hundreds of thousands of times higher than the energy per particle in a nuclear weapon. This is a different scale and is way up there when we talk about high-energy physics.

That sounds dangerous.

Not really. If you stood in the beam at CERN, it would probably kill you. But, things in a steel factory can kill you too. If you're referring to weapons applications, it's something entirely different than what you might be thinking. In a nuclear weapon, you're taking matter and making energy. At CERN, it goes the other way. They're taking energy and making matter. I don't think it's dangerous and I don't see any practical applications for it. I just think we need to know. We need to know what's going on and we have the ability. If you need to know and you have the ability, you do it. It's money well spent. It's exactly like the exploration of space with satellites and probes.

There are a lot of parallels.

It is all connected. The same laws of physics apply in the tiny, white-hot early universe and the coldest, vastest expanses of outer space. In terms of enterprises, they are also similar. They influence each other. Modern cosmology has had a bearing on elementary particle physics and elementary particle physics has had a bearing on cosmology. The fact that these two are related is kind of amazing. They inform each other, and the knowledge is valuable because it is knowledge about the true nature of things. I don't see a downside. It is good and important to do bold work in new areas.

Interviewed 9/26/06

LARISSA HARRIS

Associate Director of the Center for Advanced Visual Studies

What are you working on here at MIT?

I'm the associate director of an art organization called the Center for Advanced Visual Studies. Since its establishment in 1967, CAVS has been a center for art making here at MIT. I came onboard in July 2004 and have instituted several new programs. One is a visitor series intended to raise our profile, create an audience, and generate interest in what we do here. The second is a long-term fellowship program which is where artists come for a year or more and make a new project at MIT, with people from MIT. Another is a local artist's program which provides studios for selected promising young local artists and, finally, there is something we call the Graduate Affiliate Program in which MIT students—graduate students who are also artists—get a studio from us so they can work out their artistic visions on our turf. We provide them a place to do that and they provide a link back to their own departments for the visitors, the fellows, and the locals.

The way the visits work is that the artists come for a couple of days and we try to give them a really good impression of what MIT is about. We set up meetings with labs, give them tours, and basically try to match-make based on what we know about them and what we had talked about prior to the visit. They present their work to our audiences and at the end of the year we ask them for a proposal for a longer project. That then is the pool from which we select the fellows.

So, in terms of what the relationship of the Center is to the rest of MIT, we are first and foremost an art making organization. We are not an art and technology making organization. The people we bring in are artists. Naturally though, the proposals we receive have interesting and provocative takes on MIT as a site. And that's what we're looking for, somebody who is interested in coming here, contributing to the culture, and either raising questions we think aren't raised often enough or reframing ideas that can use reframing. MIT as an institution is a tremendously exciting place for artists because when they come here, they can just smell that everybody else is working on crazy ideas too. Because MIT is an organization populated by makers, artists—who are makers themselves—feel quite comfortable here. Of course, people always ask, "Why here? Why art at MIT?" We constantly have to justify our existence. But as they get to know us, they come to realize why. It's actually a natural fit.

LARISSA HARRIS

What changes in the recent past, in and around your field, have affected your work?

I'll say two things. First I'll say something about being a curator—which is what I am—
—and then I'll say something about how artists are generally working. A curator, in the
conventional sense of the term, is someone who organizes exhibitions. I don't actually
organize exhibitions. We don't do exhibitions. So what do I do? I co-produce work, which
is to say, I put together the resources in the community that help artists produce a new
work. Because of the changes in the art world over the last 40 years, this has become
one of the defining duties of a curator. The responsibilities of the job have broadened,
and so defining it requires a combination of terms. It's part psychologist, financier, interior
decorator, and matchmaker.

What has precipitated these changes?

Well, the other part of my response is about the changes in contemporary art. They
extend from conceptual art, which is the notion that art is not necessarily an object but an
idea that can take any form, from text to balloons in the air. When artists were making
things they alone could make, i.e. paintings and sculptures, the curator was a different
figure. In that paradigm, the job of the curator was to think about the relationship of those
paintings and sculptures to the other paintings and sculptures of the artist, and about the
relationship between those paintings and sculptures to the paintings and sculptures of
other artists. This is a very legitimate practice, and it continues. But now, for example,
if an artist wants to make a video, or a theater-based project, or an exhibition, or a book,
or a ceramic elephant, or a circus, or a party, these things require more people. Mine is
not just an organizational position. I bring all my knowledge of contemporary art to bear,
because in conversations with artists the work grows. We hope.

Do you see yourself as a collaborator?

Sometimes, it really depends on the piece. I see myself as a facilitator. Some of
the things I didn't mention in my list of jobs for the curator would be P.T. Barnum-like
impresario, promoter, and translator. To do all these jobs extremely well is impossible,
so you focus your energies where you can and you bring other people in to help. We
have two part-time staff members, Joe Zane and Meg Rotzel, who are essential to the
production process. It is they who are in closet proximity to each project as it develops.
I check in regularly, but tend to focus more on the bigger picture, which means
developing the overall vision, thinking about who could be our next happy match, and

keeping the money flowing in.

What role do you think your work is playing in a larger global context and how do you see it developing in the future?

The art world is international already, so it is incumbent upon us at this center to produce work that is seen internationally. Contributing to culture is not as easily quantified as contributing to cancer research. Art is a living, changing system of belief that I feel has the capacity to change the way people look at the world. I'm not ambitious about making art bigger in order to make more people see things differently. I think of art as a subjective experience for an individual, and I try to keep that in mind when I'm thinking about where the art we make here will go.

What are the implications of the implementation of your work? Are there downsides?

People accuse art of being useless. I suppose that's a downside. But there's a place for uselessness in the world, for sure. If I had to, I would say that the use of art is to shift one's perceptions of the world, even for a second. I won't deny that it's too often a practice and experience reserved only for the elite, or for certain people who know certain codes and have access to certain places. But one of the things about this program I am so proud of is that we're ignoring those assumptions about art and we are saying that this experience is available for anybody who is interested. We are demonstrating here, by our very existence, that art has a fundamental place everywhere in life—as a companion to science and technology, as a companion to architecture, and as a vital part of the human experience.

Interviewed 5/8/07

HENRY S. MARCUS

Professor of Marine Systems
Chairman of the Oceans System Management Program

What are you working on here at MIT?

I am the Chairman of the Ocean Systems Management Program. We focus primarily on marine transportation systems. However, that can only be done effectively if one looks at the overall logistics system, which includes everything that happens with a piece of cargo from the point of origin to the final destination. Addressing all of these issues requires the application of skill sets ranging from engineering to management, economics, policy, and law. In a recent project, we were analyzing taking coal from the middle of the United States, putting it on barges, bringing it down the Mississippi, taking it off the barges, putting it on land-based terminals, and then reloading it onto ocean-going vessels to carry it across the Gulf of Mexico and beyond. The planning, coordination, and execution of this type of operation goes far beyond engineering and requires a comprehensive understanding and implementation of information technology.

Have there been any considerable changes or developments in the recent past that have affected your work?

There are changes occurring constantly that affect our work. From a logistical point of view, we have three main tasks—moving the cargo, moving the information that is needed to move the cargo, and moving the money. Each of these areas is changing all the time, in different ways and at different rates. For example, the ships are getting much bigger and faster, but the ports are not evolving quickly enough to handle these ships. So, the ability to move cargo in and out of the ports is not keeping pace with the other links in the chain. Additionally, because there is now increased emphasis on security and environmental protection, we have to be more concerned with identification tags for tracking and tracing, global positioning systems, and the enforcement of all the environmental regulations. It's a constant challenge, but that's what makes it so fascinating.

Can you elaborate on the issues of port security and environmental protection?

With port security, the real trick is to be able to implement a system which not only improves security, but also commercially and economically benefits the ship owners, those in the logistical system, and the ports. People have to want to make these changes. They

have to want to invest in them. They have to see the tangible benefits in improving the system. Unfortunately, so far there's been a disconnect. Port security and commercial improvements are being pursued as separate ends unto themselves. There has not been much overlap, and that hurts both systems. At MIT, we've been trying to address this, but it's not an easy problem to solve.

Regarding the environment, if you look specifically at oil spills, there's been great improvement since the Exxon Valdez spill in 1989. We had the Oil Pollution Act of 1990, and we've seen significant changes in the designs of vessels—for instance, double hulled tankers. Plus, companies worldwide are doing a much better job of training people. That's helped tremendously because more than 80% of all accidents are caused by human error. The amount of oil spilled has decreased considerably, but it's a constant concern and we still have more to do.

How has the recent emphasis on emissions and global warming affected the field?

Recently, we have seen more emphasis on topics like ship air emissions, and less on oil spills. Some ship owners would like to use higher quality fuel, and they have promoted a worldwide agreement to that end. However, it is not clear whether we can produce enough fuel of that quality to actually stem emissions in a meaningful way. And as you keep pushing ahead, you need better engine technology, better exhaust systems, and perhaps even several different fuel tanks aboard ships in order to use different quality fuels in different places. Ship design, and the entire system around it, is becoming more and more complicated. We need policy changes on an international level, but there are constant disagreements among the countries—and even among states within the U.S.— regarding what the policies will be and how they will be enforced. There are many things one might like to do, but the reality is that all change is influenced by economics.

What role does your work play in a global context and how do you envision the future of your field?

Our key role is to train the managers of the future to work in this industry. Whether in the government or commercial sector, that means grooming people who have a background in both engineering and ocean systems management skills. I've been here for 36 years, and in that time, I'm proud to say, we've trained and placed people all around the world, working for shipping companies, ship builders, ports, and various government agencies.

What issues will you and people like you have to address in the coming decades?

For industrialized nations, the main problem will be capacity. The growth rate has been tremendous. It takes only a few years to build bigger, better, faster, greener ships, but it takes many, many years to build the port facilities, the rail facilities, and the roadway network to be able to properly handle that traffic. As far as this is concerned, the United States has difficult problems ahead.

What are the implications of your work? Are there downsides?

You get up in the morning, the alarm clock or clock radio goes off, you put on your clothes, you turn on the coffee machine, you drink your coffee, you eat a banana, you use the microwave, you turn on the TV to see what the news is—everything you've touched has been on a ship. Our standard of living, and the standard of living in all the advanced nations, depends on efficient marine transportation systems and efficient overall logistical systems. Improvements in these systems are necessary. Having said that, if you speak to everyday people, you'll see that there is absolutely no appreciation of how much each one of us depends on marine transportation. Unfortunately, if people don't understand and embrace this issue soon, our ports will become so clogged that we will be unable to efficiently transport the cargo. Then it will be much too late. I've been on the Marine Transportation Systems National Advisory Council and other advisory groups that have tried to address this issue and, believe me, it's an incredible challenge to alter people's thinking and awareness.

What do we need to understand?

People have to understand how important marine transportation is to our nation, to globalization, and to the world. Any single item in your house might have parts from five different countries. It takes an incredibly efficient system to manufacture this item, transport it, and deliver it swiftly to the consumer at a reasonable price. Our standard of living is dependent upon the smooth functioning of this system. It's a long, hard sell though, and both the government and the entire maritime industry continue to fight this battle of awareness. If we want to at least maintain our status quo, we must pay attention before the crisis arrives. Otherwise, the loss of an efficient transportation/logistics system is going to be difficult and painful.

Interviewed 5/15/07

LAWRENCE J. VALE

Professor of Urban Design and Planning
Head of the Department of Urban Studies and Planning

What are you working on here at MIT?

For many years, my basic interest has been what I call design politics. This means trying to understand the relationship between two ideas that people often keep separate: a sense that the world, specifically an urban environment, is designed, and the concurrent reality that it is shaped by social, political, and cultural processes. At the confluence of these areas, there is much to learn about relationships of power and questions of identity. By examining the meaning of the built environment, we have access to this knowledge. This investigation is my way of understanding something about what makes the world the way it is.

One project I'm working on right now is an attempt to do a second edition of a book I wrote in 1992. It is called *Architecture, Power, and National Identity,* and it is a look at parliamentary complexes and designed capital cities in a variety of countries around the world. It investigates the meaning of the nation-state as expressed through the built environment. I'm revisiting it fifteen years later to see how some of the places have changed.

I also spent most of the 1990's writing about the design, history, and politics of American public housing—that is, the formal way in which we in the United States have tried to house the least advantaged citizens. The first book, *From the Puritans to the Projects,* was a look back to the early days of Boston in the early part of the 17th century and the attitudes about where the poor should be housed. It then follows the evolution of those attitudes all the way through various issues with immigration and into the public housing projects of the mid and late 20th century. So the book became a history of the Boston Housing Authority, but also a look at race and poverty and the variety of ways people have struggled to cope with those issues spatially. Then there was a sequel called *Reclaiming Public Housing.* That book was about efforts to rebuild and reinvest in public housing in ways that could be supportive of the low-income communities that live there. My current work is an attempt to take that project, which had been focused on Boston, and expand it by looking at some examples of how public housing has been transformed in several other cities nationwide.

Most recently, what has taken up most of my time is an edited book I did called *The Resilient City.* That is about how modern cities recover from disaster. For better or worse, the book came out the week of the Asian tsunami at the end of December 2004. So there was a spate of relevance at that point, and then the book was in its bookstore visibility right when Hurricane Katrina hit New Orleans. Therefore, I've spent a lot of my time since the end of August 2005 trying to see what my work has to say about the processes of recovery and what the nature of recovery means in a place like the devastated gulf coast of the United States.

To me, these three areas are all, at some level, connected to the politics of design. The early work on nationalism and capitals, the public housing work, and the work on disasters and disaster recovery are all part of the same exploration.

What changes in and around your field in the recent past have affected your research today?

I think one thing that has happened is that more and more people are starting to make connections between the socio-political side of the built environment and the aesthetic side, so there is more work to keep track of. I certainly welcome that opportunity, but it makes it more difficult for someone like me, who works on several topics, to keep fully abreast of what goes on in my field. The other thing that, of course, has made a huge difference is the electronic availability of so much material. It has become possible to monitor more of what is going on while remaining in one place. That has been enormously helpful.

I think recently there has been greater recognition that these kinds of symbolic questions about the built environment, that have always interested me, are actually very powerful. So when something like the World Trade Center attacks happen, where the attack is not simply an attack on a building but an attack on symbols of Western values and Western capitalism, it drives home the issues that I've been talking about for many years. We look at the built environment as a proxy for our values, and the things we build and rebuild are in response to our inability to resolve issues on a direct human to human level. In other words, we somehow transmit meaning into the built world.

Where do you see your work in a global context? Where do you see it going?

I find it hard to separate my own research agenda from my role as head of the Urban

Studies and Planning Department because, really, we play an institutional role on a global scale that is very different from most departments. Because my own work has engaged six continents and I'm very interested in the global scale of these issues, it comes naturally to me. We are the largest department of urban planning in the United States, the oldest continuous one, and one of the few in the United States that really works on every continent on issues of urban planning and development.

I think the main significance of being here at MIT is that we are welcomed in the far corners of the globe as an honest broker of reason and good sense about problems that are both global and, by definition, local. We are now establishing systematic partnerships with key institutions at a variety of locales in places where we see the challenges of urbanization as particularly acute. It is one thing to worry about the problems of suburban sprawl in the United States, which we certainly have faculty members addressing, but it is also necessary to recognize that as a planet we are now, for the first time, more than 50% urbanized and moving further in that direction ever more rapidly. I'm in the process of finishing a chart, that will go on a wall here at MIT, that is a long timeline of global urbanization, looking back just a couple of hundred years ago when only 3% of the planet lived in cities, to a point in 1950 where it was still only 30%, to a time in 2030 where we'll be 60% urbanized. This is a massive global transformation that has occurred, of course, in the United States, but more dramatically in places like China, India and other countries that were rural, agrarian societies and are being pushed rapidly into the industrialized 21st century with all of the implications for energy use, climate change, and global sustainability.

So I see our work, not just my own, as trying to speak to the global extent of the problems that we study. It does no good to simply focus on one's backyard. Although that is important, we as a national and international institution have a particular responsibility to engage as fully as possible in what we recognize as the great global problems of urban development and urbanization, and not simply ones that may be particular to the New England region or to the region around any university. We are trying to be as engaged as possible, in a focused way, in the places where we can put together the critical mass and the quality of partnerships to make a long-term difference in the lives of people and the conditions of places.

What are the implications of your work? Is there a downside?

Right now I would say that the limitations of my work and, more generally, the work of urban planning scholars and practitioners is that we are frequently in a society—for example, here in the United States—that does not value the systematic planning of environments and environmental change. We are faced with this challenge of how to deal with fundamental transformations in the quality of life in the context of an active democratic polity. We often look to other places that have found ways to plan more systematically, but we must temper our admiration for that with the recognition that much of what gets done in other places is done in an unacceptable top-down manner that gives no adequate voice to the range of public opinion that should be heard and considered. So, the greatest challenge in our field is what we call planning action, which means not simply being able to come up with a plan for the future, but to come up with a plausible mode of implementation for what we see as important, so that it can be transmitted and realized through a democratic process.

The downside is that we will be lone voices in a disappearing wilderness as the consequences of this global urbanization multiply and not only impede the ability of people to conduct their lives in an efficient manner, but also threaten the very viability of the planet. If we don't figure out the challenges of transportation, energy, housing and equitable sharing of a number of urban amenities, we are headed for a time when cities will be economically unsustainable and, as a result, national economies will suffer.

Interviewed 2/7/06

KERRY A. EMANUEL

Professor of Atmospheric Science

What are you working on at MIT?

Broadly speaking, my research is on atmospheres and climate. I'm interested in matters such as atmosphere water vapor, which is the most important greenhouse gas and is largely controlled by very detailed physical processes going on inside clouds. I'm also interested in all kinds of tropical weather systems that at present are poorly understood, such as oscillations of the equatorial region that occur on time scales of a few days to as much as sixty days, and in hurricanes.

My philosophy, and it's the philosophy that runs through this department, is to use all available tools to understand a phenomenon. In other words, rather than beginning with a method and then looking for ways to apply it, I try instead to focus on understanding a particular process by using every tool at my disposal. In this field, that means basic theory, laboratory experiments, computer modeling of systems, and it means occasionally going into the field to collect data in real systems.

Can you tell us what you've found regarding hurricanes?

Hurricanes are controlled by fluxes of heat from the ocean to the atmosphere and by the drag the atmosphere exerts on the hurricane. But there are many different things going on in these systems that are not very well understood. It's a very difficult phenomenon to model because there are critical processes occurring on scales of a few hundred meters or less. At the same time, a domain size of perhaps one thousand kilometers is required to capture the phenomenon as a whole. So you're talking about a computationally intensive problem. However, I prefer problem solving systems that favor cleverly designed models, rather than the brute force approach of computer power.

There are very complex issues regarding the interface of air and sea. Virtually everything that controls hurricane intensity takes place in a remarkably small region under the eyewall. This region is an annulus that is maybe ten kilometers thick and thirty kilometers in diameter. The main processes that control the intensity are the evaporation of the seawater in that region and the drag the sea exerts on the atmosphere. We do understand now how to formulate those transfers at low wind speeds because we have

solid theory and good experimental field data. However, at high wind speeds it's a different problem. The entire air/sea interface becomes an emulsion. Topologically, there is no surface. Bubble-filled water transitions gradually to spray-filled air. This is almost impossible to model numerically. Therefore, to figure out what's happening there, we've been doing laboratory experiments and have been trying to make measurements in real hurricanes.

What changes in the recent past have affected your research today?

Well there are technical changes, political changes, and scientific changes. Technically, the advent of high-speed computing has really changed the field. That's probably true in many fields. Meteorology has always been a computer-intensive discipline. Ever since the advent of computers, we've always taken the fastest one and pushed it to its limits. If you were to look at the sales statistics of super computers, I think you would find that the two biggest clients are the atmospheric science and defense fields.

There are other advances that have been predicated upon advances in satellites and satellite instrumentation. I don't work much in that area myself. And, of course, the field has been altered because of the enormous concern about global warming and the pressure put on people like me to understand how it works.

Do you share the concern?

Yes. Fifty years ago, we had only a body of theory to rely on. Climate models had not yet been invented, it was too early to see changes in the observations, and paleo-climatology hadn't yet achieved a detailed record of what happened during the ice ages. The theory that existed then already had some uncertainties to deal with—such as, the response of clouds to climate change. Since that time, the theory has gotten better, climate models have come online, and the paleo-data have become more precise and extensive. Most importantly, a signal has emerged unambiguously from the background variability of climate. There's no doubt in my mind, and in the minds of almost all my colleagues, that we're experiencing a manmade global warming effect now.

How does it affect hurricanes? How have the hurricanes changed recently?

Based on the work that we did in the 1980's, we thought that we would see a modest change of about 5% in wind speed for every degree of raised ocean temperature. That's small but detectable. But a few years ago we found that hurricanes—at least those in the Atlantic—have been responding somewhat more sensitively than we had predicted. We've been trying to grapple with that discrepancy, and have made some progress. Part of the reason for the disparity is that the theory only dealt with the wind speed itself, whereas the observational analysis calculated the power of hurricanes over their lifetimes, which also depends on how many storms occur and how long they last. The number of storms has been increasing and they have been lasting longer. But there are other things going on. The cooling of the lower stratosphere, which also contributes to the increase in hurricane intensity, was not predicted. It is definitely happening and we're not sure why. That's one of the questions researchers are attacking at the moment.

Where do you see your work in a global context and where do you see it going in the future?

Obviously, there's practical concern with how hurricanes respond to climate. We're developing tools that allow us, without actually having to simulate hurricanes, to assess risk in any given climate. We're also trying to get a handle on exactly what large-scale climate factors control hurricane activity. We really don't understand what controls rates of hurricane formation.

Although not often talked about, hurricanes themselves may have a profound effect on climate. It is a two-way problem, not just a one-way problem. Hurricanes churn up the uppermost few hundred meters of the ocean, and this turns out to be very important to the climate system. Thermodynamically, the surface of the tropical oceans is cooled, but, paradoxically, the depths become warmer. Ocean currents then carry the warm water poleward, making it warmer at higher latitudes, and a bit cooler at lower latitudes, than the Earth might otherwise be.

A lot of stock is being placed in global climate models for future predictions. But global climate models don't have meaningful hurricanes. They have very, very weak, fake hurricanes. And because they don't have real hurricanes, they cannot address the effect of hurricanes on the climate system.

So that's a variable that hasn't been included?

That's right. This idea that hurricanes have an important effect on climate is new. Part of the problem is persuading climate scientists that this may be important.

KERRY A. EMANUEL

What are the implications of your work? Are there downsides?

If there are big increases in hurricane activity due to global warming, there could be profound consequences. We saw what Hurricane Katrina did. The U.S. can't afford too many more events like that. Furthermore, if there is exaggerated high latitude warming, it could increase the risk of melting continental ice, such as in Greenland. That would, in turn, increase sea level.

Are you involved in policy making or policy recommendations?

No, not really. I stay out of that for two reasons. First, it's not my forte. I don't think I'd be good at it. Second, I believe scientists must resist the urge to become advocates. It compromises one's objectivity, or at least the appearance of objectivity, which is sometimes as important as the actual objectivity. On the other hand, there is no reason why we can't provide advice to people who are serious about policy. I do that all the time.

In what capacity?

Anything from testifying to congress about the state of research, to pushing government and non-government groups to seriously address the demographic problem of coastal developments in the United States. But even if it's clear that a policy has to change, I try to refrain from making suggestions as to how it should change.

Mine is a campaign of information. I've spent a lot of time, in fact an inordinate amount of time, in the last year and a half or so—whether through seminars, newspaper articles, or interviews—just communicating to the public. I think I sound like a broken record, but there are people who don't get it.

Interviewed 11/13/06

JOHN STERMAN

Jay W. Forrester Professor of Management
Director of the MIT System Dynamics Group

What are you working on here at MIT?

We build formal simulation models to help address important challenges in business and public policy. But before I get into the details, I think I should first say a few words about system dynamics. System dynamics is an interdisciplinary field that was created here at MIT by Jay Forrester. Jay's background was in engineering and, unlike some theorists who simply write about how complex systems work, he actually worked as an engineer on important real world projects such as stabilizing radar systems on ships in the Second World War and developing computer systems for strategic air defense. So he came to the table with a very pragmatic attitude, largely conditioned by his experience growing up on a cattle ranch in western Nebraska, where if you didn't fix something yourself, it didn't get done.

That pragmatic attitude still characterizes our field. One of the things that attracts me to this work is that it's not roped in by the traditional disciplinary boundaries in academia. I've worked on a wide range of issues, and I've found that diversity to be not only intellectually stimulating, but also a basis for better understanding the pressing problems we face in this world.

If you think about the way business schools are organized, they are much like companies with separate departments—finance, marketing, operations, and so forth. The difficulty is that managers don't have operations problems, financial problems, and marketing problems. They just have problems. And one of the reasons they have these problems is that they continue to divide up the world into these categories. We live in a world of interaction and complexity. You can't create a high-performing organization if you're only focused on optimizing the pieces.

Can you explain how you put the data and information to use?

There is a theoretical perspective behind what we do, which is the theory of non-linear dynamics and feedback systems. This comes from engineering and mathematics. There is a beautiful and elegant mathematics underlying the models we develop. But the math isn't enough. Over the years, we've worked hard to develop tools based on these theories

that are useful in the real world of busy managers who don't have technical training, where data are often not available, and where decisions are made under time pressure. Having the mathematical tools and building formal simulation models is an essential part of our practice. They provide principles, conceptual frameworks, and a testing process that helps us improve our understanding, develop better policies, and build the broad understanding among stakeholders required for implementation and sustained success.

Tell me more.

Many well-intentioned efforts to solve problems fail, or cause new problems that we then blame on outside forces, when in fact they are the unintended consequences of our own past actions. This "policy resistance" arises because our mental models—how we understand the systems in which we are embedded—are narrow, taking only a few factors into account. We strive for a broad model boundary to be sure we capture as many of the key interactions and feedbacks as we can. This requires a wide range of data, quantitative and qualitative. One of our current projects focuses on policies to create sustainable markets for alternative fuel vehicles. We're developing models to help policy makers in state and national government, as well as auto companies and energy companies, design policies to develop transportation systems that reduce our greenhouse gas emissions. Dethroning internal combustion and gasoline, which have dominated the energy and transportation system for a hundred years now, is not easy. Many prior attempts to create such markets started well, but then fizzled out. We've developed a set of models that examine the interactions of drivers, carmakers, fuel providers, regulators, and other stakeholders to examine how successful markets for such vehicles can be created. The models are spatially explicit, dynamic, and behavioral.

Modeling such a problem is challenging because we seek to model markets that don't yet exist. No one knows which particular technologies will be best. Will it be hydrogen fuel cells, ethanol, biodiesel, plug-in hybrids, or something entirely novel? Building such a market involves multiple feedbacks. For example, no one will invest in fuel stations for alternative vehicles unless they think there's going to be a market for such cars. Meanwhile, nobody's going to buy such cars unless they know they can get fuel. How do you get started then? We need to know about the technologies, their costs, fuel availability, consumer attitudes and choice processes, driver behavior, and a wide range of other factors. How does the public become aware of the existence of alternative vehicles? How familiar with the alternatives must drivers be to consider them in their purchase decision? How fast will experience, R&D, and growing scale drive costs down?

How do energy suppliers decide when and where to locate fuel stations? How would the availability of fuel affect how much and where people drive, and how would those trips affect the demand for fuel?

A useful framework to address these issues entails a very broad model boundary and requires a wide range of data, data that are often difficult to get or may not exist—for example, how drivers might react to alternative vehicles no one can buy yet. In our modeling we seek the broadest range of data, including numerical data and qualitative data from interviews and even ethnographic field study. Then we try to triangulate. All types of data are needed to develop a good theory that is robust, useful, and holds up in the field.

We've also done work on climate change. MIT has one of the world's very best programs on the science and economics of climate change. Our work is complementary to that effort. We seek to understand and improve the mental models ordinary people have constructed about how the climate works, and why those models conflict with what the science tells us. The dynamics of the climate are exquisitely complex, but the processes through which human activity is changing the climate are clear enough now that scientific understanding is not the bottleneck preventing action to reduce greenhouse gas emissions. The bottleneck to action is public understanding.

We've done a series of experimental studies documenting how people think about the climate, why there is so little sense of urgency among the public. For example, we'll give people a description of how the climate works drawn from the Intergovernmental Panel on Climate Change's *Summary for Policymakers*—that is, from the non-technical overview of the IPCC's scientific reports intended for policymakers, the media, and citizens. We show people graphs displaying the concentration of carbon dioxide in the atmosphere, along with the flow of CO_2 emissions into the atmosphere, and the rate at which CO_2 is removed from the atmosphere as it is taken up by plants and dissolves in the ocean. We show people that only about half the emissions caused by human activity are removed each year. Then we ask, "Atmospheric concentrations of CO_2 have been growing since the start of the Industrial Revolution. Suppose we want to stabilize the concentration of CO_2. What would have to happen to emissions?" Most people, even MIT students, tell us that we need to stabilize emissions. Well, that's wrong. For the level of CO_2 in the atmosphere to stabilize, emissions of CO_2 into the atmosphere have to be exactly balanced by the removal of CO_2 from it. Since emissions are double removal, emissions have to fall by at least half, or removal has to double. Most scientists, by the way, believe removal will fall over time as the sinks currently absorbing CO_2 saturate and as more carbon in soils is released to the air by warming. But most people asked this question tell us that we can stabilize atmospheric CO_2 while also showing emissions continuously greater than removal. That, of course, is impossible. Note that you don't need any training in climatology to understand it. It's a question of accumulation. It's exactly the same as filling a bathtub. Water goes into the tub. Water goes out of the tub. For the level of water in the tub to remain constant, you have to have water draining out of the tub as fast as it's flowing in. If you put water in your bathtub faster than it drains out, the level of water in the tub will rise, and vice versa.

The result, that stabilizing atmospheric CO_2 concentrations requires very large cuts in emissions, is not dependent on anyone's climate model. It has nothing to do with what political party you're in. It's not a function of whether you're skeptical about climate change or not. It's just a question of basic accounting. People's poor understanding of the basic accumulation dynamics matters because people who think that the climate can be stabilized just by slowing the growth of emissions are likely to believe that this is not an urgent issue, that there is time, and that we can wait and see what's going to happen. Then, if it turns out that climate change is really going to hurt us, we can do something. That's completely wrong. By the time we find out how bad climate change will be, it will be too late.

Obviously, there's more going on with people's resistance to taking action to slow global warming than just their misunderstanding of the "bathtub dynamics" of the climate, but I think such misperceptions are an important barrier to action. We're never going to have scientific certainty about how much the climate is going to change until it's too late to do anything about it. What we're talking about is whether it is worth buying an insurance policy against the risk that society and the ecosystems upon which we depend will be significantly harmed by climate change. The cost of that insurance is the cost of reducing our dependence on fossil fuels, of creating a carbon-neutral economy powered by renewable energy. We would pay that insurance premium in the form of higher prices for fossil fuels through, say, a carbon tax, with the revenue used, for example, to cut income taxes, balance the budget, save social security, or fund research into renewable energy. The costs are actually not as great as people fear. Unfortunately, I think one of the reasons people aren't willing to buy this insurance by paying a little bit more for energy today is that they think there is plenty of time to wait. But the basic physics of the climate dictate that we must make the decision today.

These experiments on people's mental models of the climate have broader applicability. Our experimental studies show that most people, including experienced managers, don't understand the basic principles of accumulation, whether its CO_2 accumulating in the atmosphere, inventories accumulating in their supply chain, or high-risk mortgages accumulating on their balance sheet. As an example, suppose you're in the telecom industry and the number of subscribers to your cell phone service is not growing as fast as you would like. What should be done? Most people say you should cut prices, advertise heavily, and run promotions to get more subscribers. Well, that would give you more subscribers in the short run, but at very high customer acquisition costs because competition is so intense.

People rarely mention the higher leverage point, which is to reduce the loss of existing customers. People tend to focus on putting more in, instead of reducing the rate of loss. You can reduce the loss of existing customers by providing better service, continually staying in touch with customers' needs, and addressing the problems they're telling you they have. That, in many ways, appears to be more difficult, but it's actually cheaper in the long run than buying customers at great expense through promotions and discounts. Additionally, increasing the flow of new customers is likely to be self-defeating. If you are losing customers now because your service is poor, adding more people to your customer base increases the load on your capacity and service organization still further, ultimately forcing people out at an even faster rate and preventing your customer base from growing at all.

The challenge of building a carbon-neutral world, of creating sustainable markets for alternative vehicles, connects to another theme in our work: getting it done. These changes require the implementation of new technologies and processes, and deep transformations in organizational structure and capabilities. Our work in this area was motivated by early experiences we had studying process improvement in companies. We observed senior managers trying as hard as they could to implement improvement programs such as Total Quality Management, reengineering, lean manufacturing, and Six Sigma. One can clearly see that these tools work for some firms, such as Toyota or General Electric, where they have led to substantial improvement and competitive advantage.

Of course, everybody wanted to imitate these companies. There are hundreds of consultants, textbooks, seminars, and training workshops—resources that, in theory, should make it easy to integrate these tools into your organization. In practice, however, it is devilishly difficult, and most of the companies seeking to do so have failed. It is not unusual for employees in a company to experience half a dozen different improvement initiatives in just a few years, each of which began with great promise but failed to deliver. These failures often lead employees and managers to develop a cynical attitude about improvement programs and to become depressed about the possibility of enduring change. We see organizations stuck in what we call the firefighting trap, where, as one manager put it, "We never had time to improve or do preventive maintenance because we spent all our time trying to keep the line going." Many firms are trapped in a vicious cycle: firefighting to get product out the door takes time from improvement, which then makes it harder to get product out the door.

We've studied why this happens and what can be done about it. This has resulted in a stream of work which has been published in academic journals—because it is of interest to theorists—and that we also bring to managers because of its practical importance. We study interventions on the ground, which involves fieldwork and qualitative research, as well as data gathering and model building. We develop what we call management flight simulators, converting our models into interactive games in which participants can play the role of the decision makers, and, in many cases for the very first time, experience the long-term effects of their decisions. This is important because in the real world, we usually experience only the local and immediate effects of our decisions, which are often quite different from the long-term and distant effects.

The fastest way to put money into the bottom line is to kill research, defer maintenance, and cut training. Companies do this when they are under budget pressure. They do it thinking that when things improve, they can restart the development process, do the maintenance they've deferred, and send everyone to training. Instead, their underlying capabilities begin to erode. It doesn't happen right away, but it happens. You don't have to change the oil regularly in your car. It will still run just fine. But if you never change it, eventually you're going to blow the engine. So, in the short run it looks like there's no cost to this corner cutting, and management often rewards the apparent improvement in productivity. But gradually, slowly, inevitably, corner cutting erodes your capabilities. Performance deteriorates, breakdowns increase, and quality falls. To meet customer requirements then requires heroic effort, further disrupting operations as people helping to put out the fire are unavailable to do maintenance or invest time in process improvement or innovation. Costs rise, unhappy customers leave, revenues decline, and you have to cut back still more on improvement, maintenance, research, training, and so on. This happens inadvertently and subtly at first, but can become a death spiral that traps an organization in a state of perpetual turbulence, firefighting, low morale, customer churn, and employee turnover.

Understanding the firefighting trap, as a concept, is straightforward. Documenting it is easy, because it's so common. Getting people to take action, and actually get out of the trap, is hard. When you do the right thing, the first consequence is that costs rise and performance drops. This is because resources must be diverted from firefighting and working harder, and applied toward the new goals of overall improvement and working smarter. Only later will you see the benefits in higher quality, reliability, and performance. Performance has to get worse before it gets better. Many managers don't understand why this is so, and, caught by surprise when it happens, don't have the stomach for this worse-before-better dynamic. They conclude that the improvement techniques they are trying to implement must not really work. Subsequently, they abandon them. So, in our research, we focus on the people who have been able to overcome the firefighting trap successfully. We study their vision for their organization, how they articulate their values, the learning processes, performance metrics, incentives, and other support resources needed for success. Interestingly, many people feel that you have to have senior management support to succeed, but many senior managers will often say they can't invest in improvement, or can't risk suffering that worse-before-better dynamic, because of pressure from Wall Street. Even more interesting, while it's often useful to have senior management support, it's frequently unnecessary. Some of the most successful applications have been in settings where the policies, attitudes, and behaviors supporting improvement grew organically, rising up from the very bottom of the organization.

Firefighting isn't just a corporate phenomenon. From the collapse of bridges to the health care crisis, our society is trapped in the vicious cycle of firefighting. Some former students are working with the Centers for Disease Control and Prevention on chronic diseases including diabetes, obesity, and hypertension. Diabetes is an epidemic in our society now, and around the world. The chief policies in place to respond are earlier diagnosis through broader screening—particularly of poor and minority groups who don't have access to quality health care—and better treatment for those who are diagnosed. Once diagnosed, interventions, including bringing people's blood sugar under control, can reduce the progression of the disease, limit complications, and save lives. These are important policies, and we have an ethical duty to treat all those in need.

But if you look at the data, the prevalence of diabetes in the United States has been going up very rapidly, despite these policies. The CDC has, several times, gone through the exercise of setting goals calling for dramatic reductions in prevalence. They have consistently failed. Prevalence keeps going up. Why? First, the more successfully we screen and diagnose, and the more successfully people are treated, the larger the population diagnosed with and living with diabetes will be. Second, and more important, as the burden of diabetes and other chronic diseases grows, the cost of treatment rises, cutting the funds and health care resources available for prevention. Hospitals faced with growing costs from patients suffering the complications of chronic diseases must cut costs elsewhere. Often this means cutting the wellness programs and laying off the nurse practitioners who work with the community to address the risk factors for obesity, diabetes, and hypertension. As prevention declines, more people become ill, more show up in the emergency room with complications, and costs rise ever faster, squeezing programs for prevention still more.

The U.S. spends more on health care than any other nation in the world, yet we don't even rank in the top 30 nations in life expectancy and infant mortality. More than 45 million people have no health insurance, and the number of unhealthy days we experience is rising. As a nation, we are like the firm that defers maintenance to cut costs, only to find more equipment breaking down, which further raises costs and makes maintenance even harder. Reversing this spiral is even more difficult in health care than in a company. The delays are longer and there are more competing stakeholders, including insurers, doctors, pharmaceutical companies, and patient advocacy groups. Further, prevention is often viewed as medicating people for life, to, for example, control their high cholesterol with statins, or limit their heart attack risk with anti-clotting agents. These treatments surely have a role, but they are not true prevention. They are costly fixes applied after people are overweight or obese, have high cholesterol, or high blood pressure. They are a form of firefighting that steals resources from true prevention.

True prevention means investing in wellness programs—even though it might raise hospital costs in the short run, it will lower them much more in the long run. It means addressing our sedentary life style and poor diet—which is to say, getting the junk food and soda out of our schools, building more sidewalks and bike lanes, and making it safe to walk on the sidewalks so kids can walk or ride a bike to school instead of being driven. It means pricing gasoline high enough so people will choose to walk and ride bicycles when possible. We are now working with the CDC and some state public health agencies and hospitals to implement policies for true prevention.

The work on alternative vehicles, climate, health, and organizational transformation is part of a bigger initiative to take sustainability seriously in our curriculum. Of course, one of the problems is defining what is meant by sustainability. It's a terribly overused and misunderstood concept. It's not merely about environmental issues. Concern for the health of the environment is often framed as being in opposition to concern for the health of the economy—loggers versus spotted owls, growth versus green. Instead, each requires the other. The economy cannot exist without a healthy environment, and the environment cannot remain healthy if people have no jobs. We can't have a sustainable world if billions live in poverty and are denied basic human rights, while others fly around in Gulfstreams from one gated compound to another, rich beyond measure. We can't have a sustainable world if we strive for material success with such vigor that there is little time for family, spirituality, connection to others, and commitment to community.

To explore these ideas, we launched a new class this past spring that we call S-Lab (the Laboratory for Sustainable Business). It was an experiment in every way. It was co-taught by eight faculty members from all areas of the school in a collaborative fashion. The students came from Sloan and every other school at MIT. The students worked together in teams with real organizations on difficult challenges in their quest to build sustainable practices and products. Project sponsors ranged from small nonprofits and startups to large multinational firms and institutions such as the World Bank. It was an amazing experience. The students here are incredibly talented, hard working, and not concerned merely with their own personal success. There is an enormous appetite among our students to make a difference and to be of service, not just to chase a dollar.

What changes in the recent past, in and around your field, have affected your research?

The biggest and most obvious change is that computing power continues to grow exponentially, and this makes it possible to build models and simulations that are not only more complex, but also analyzed more richly than ever before. Your cell phone now has thousands and thousands of times more computing power than the biggest mainframe available when I started working in this field. We can do things today in simulation—such as agent-based modeling, spatial modeling, and sensitivity analysis—that we could only dream of thirty years ago. That has been absolutely wonderful. But it's very far from sufficient because if you only do that, you've built bigger models, but your cognitive constraints haven't changed. So you understand less and less until the models are just as complex and difficult to understand as the real world.

Along with improvements in hardware and software, there have been significant changes in perspective and the modeling process. This means focusing on how models should be built and the role of interaction with the client or audience. I'll tell you a quick story. One of my former students was contacted once by an executive in a company who said, "We have a big problem. Would you come build a model for us?" And he said, "No." He said no because if he goes in, listens to them describe the issue, and then builds the model, he's the one who is going to learn about the issue. He's the one who is going to internalize the lessons, not the decision makers or employees whose behavior has to change. And when he reports his findings, no one will believe them because they won't have gone through that learning process themselves. So he said, "What I am willing to do is come down and be a facilitator and a coach for you and your team to develop the model." This is a huge change in process. First of all, it works much better. It still fails sometimes, but the other way never works. The only hope for sustained implementation success is for the decision makers themselves to go through the learning process. They are the people who need to change their modes of thinking and behavior in order for things to improve. That means that, in some meaningful way, they have to become the modelers.

That's been a substantial and difficult change. You know, if a faster computer comes around, we all know how to deal with that. But shifting from being the expert to being the facilitator cuts the wrong way for a lot of academics. They either can't do it, or they're not good at it even if they want to do it. This has meant big changes in the nature of doctoral education, for example. We still require all the Ph.D. students in our program to take classes from the Engineering School or the Math Department in control theory and non-linear dynamics. They have to understand those subjects deeply and well. But they also need to study ethnography, field research methods, and organizational behavior. They must also develop their facilitation skills and skills as catalysts of organizational transformation. That requires breadth of talent and creates some cognitive dissonance for many people. It's often uncomfortable, but it's necessary if we are to have sustained beneficial impact, if we are to build the capacity in others to think systemically rather than increasing their dependence on outside experts. Of course, I am personally still struggling to develop my own skills in these areas as well.

Another change relates to the growth of the field. System dynamics is relatively new. There aren't that many people around who do it. There's a larger number now but still a fairly small set of first-rate centers in universities where you can get a terrific education. But the field is growing. There's a professional society, journals, and annual conferences.

All these things are attracting more and more people. Participation, membership, and publications are all growing at the rate of 7% to 10% a year. That's just about the maximum growth rate that I think can be sustained while maintaining quality.

There is a challenge as more companies and organizations are becoming aware that the tools and methods currently available are not only failing to solve the problems they face, but in many cases are making them worse. People seek a systemic approach, they want a participatory approach, and they need tools to help them understand complexity. There is increasing demand, but the risk is that the demand growth will outstrip the growth in capacity. If that happens, quality declines because people enter who aren't skilled, oversight of projects deteriorates, and you get poor outcomes. That dynamic can kill companies and significantly hurt a field. So, in the last fifteen years we've had to pay attention to the problems posed by success, and it's a continuing challenge.

Where do you see your work in a global context and where do you see it going?

I first found out about system dynamics through my father, who is a research chemist. I was still in high school at the time. Then I went to college in New Hampshire in order to ski as much as possible. On the side, outside of classes, I was studying systems and building models. One day a friend came to me and said, "You know, there's something just like what you're messing around with in the mainframe public library." It turned out that two of the key people in the field, who had been trained here at MIT, had just joined the faculty there. It was one of those serendipities you can't possibly plan, but decisively affects your life. I changed my major and took every class they offered. Most of the work I did then was focused on the challenges of global environmental sustainability.

So now I'm here at the Management School and some people say, "Well that's a strange place. Why would you want to do that when you could be in an environmental studies program or in public policy?" System dynamics started here at MIT. MIT has students of tremendous capability, and with the curiosity, work ethic, and commitment to these issues to make a difference. That makes it exciting to be here. Further, large business enterprises are the most important institutions in the world today. They control the most resources, they command the most time from our citizens, and they have the most influence on the political process. If we're going to create a sustainable society, we have to work with those organizations. We also have to work with the people who are going to be the leaders of those organizations, and those future leaders are the students here.

Most of our research projects, by the way, are carried out by Ph.D. students and post docs, Masters students, and even undergrads, through the Undergraduate Research Opportunities Program (UROP). That's really exciting for me. One of the great things about being at MIT is learning from others, including the students.

What are the implications of your work? Do you see a downside?

Modeling, not just system dynamics modeling, but all forms of computer-based modeling——econometrics, optimization, agent-based simulation, all forms of computer-based analysis—have had an aura around them. It is diminishing a bit as people become more computer savvy, but it's still there. It is an aura of authority that the opinion of an expert doesn't carry. That's a very dangerous thing. Since the very beginning, we've been very concerned with the process of model testing. Models should not be black boxes with inscrutable assumptions buried in complex computer code that only a few people understand. How do you document a model properly so that any third party can replicate your results and extend and critique your work? How do you detect errors in models? Computer-based modeling in all fields has had a disappointing record in terms of how much impact it has had. Many great analyses merely sit on shelves gathering dust, while in other cases models are used despite significant errors because the assumptions are hidden, either inadvertently or deliberately.

For example, one model—a hybrid optimization-econometric model—was designed to look at how the U.S. economy could recover from a nuclear attack. This was done in the 1970's, during the Cold War. The modelers concluded that the economy would recover very quickly after a full-scale attack by the Soviets, and this conclusion was used to argue that we needed even more warheads and missiles to provide a credible deterrent. Well, the modelers assumed that our capital stock—the housing, factories, buildings, ports, roads, refineries, and all other infrastructure needed to run the economy—could be replenished with a two-year time delay. Two years is about how long it takes to build new facilities, so this assumption seemed reasonable to them, I suppose. But after a massive nuclear attack that kills perhaps a hundred million people, there isn't going to be a construction industry, there isn't going to be a highway network, and there aren't going to be energy sources to power the cement and steel industries, not to mention the labor needed to rebuild. They assumed the economy could be rebuilt without regard for the effects of the very attack they sought to model.

It sounds ridiculous that such an error could be made, but I don't think it's entirely a failing of the modelers. The policymakers and others who commissioned and reviewed the model didn't have the skills in model testing to pick that up, the model documentation was difficult to understand, and the process for its development didn't encourage open discussion of its assumptions. There are dozens of other similar examples, where models are used in a protective mode, to push an agenda, boost the authority of the modelers, and get more resources. Models should instead be used as tools to promote inquiry, to learn, and to empower people. A great deal more work needs to be done to educate policymakers and the general public about models and how they can best serve human needs.

My strong personal view is that modeling is too important to be left to the experts. Many scientists and experts believe that the major problems we face—whether it's climate change, overfishing, or traffic congestion—are all technical problems that can be solved with an approach akin to the Manhattan Project. In other words, the technical experts and senior leaders believe that if they're given enough money and left alone, they'll come up with the technology that will solve the problem. However, most of the problems that threaten humanity today are not solvable that way. In fact, many of these problems arose as the unintended consequences of prior technical solutions. Building more highways causes people to drive more and live farther out in the suburbs, worsening traffic congestion. There's no technical solution for climate change, overfishing, or traffic jams. Certainly, success requires all the creativity and technical innovation we can muster, but it requires much more as well. Success requires deep changes in the beliefs and behaviors of millions of people. Rather than the Manhattan Project, I think a better analogy is the civil rights movement. There is no technical solution for racism. Progress in that area has required changing the thinking and behavior of millions of people. It required leadership at every level of society. Support from political leaders came afterwards, and laws, institutions, and technology co-evolved with changing behaviors and attitudes. Similarly, halting climate change requires millions of individuals deciding to ride a bike or drive an efficient car instead of a gas-guzzling SUV, and supporting higher prices for carbon energy today to avoid the risk of harm to future generations tomorrow. Our political leaders will enact those policies when enough people understand the connections that bind us to one another, to the ecosystems upon which we depend, and to the future.

Interviewed 11/7/06

ERNEST J. MONIZ

Cecil and Ida Green Professor of Physics
Co-Director of the Laboratory for Energy and the Environment

What are you working on here at MIT?

My work focuses on addressing the energy and environmental challenges for the 21st century. There are three major issues. Firstly, there is tremendous pressure to increase the energy supply. Even with substantially increased energy efficiency, there will be a doubling of primary energy demand and perhaps a tripling of electricity use by mid-century. That is quite substantial, particularly when one understands that we currently have a completely fossil fuel dominated energy infrastructure and that, historically, the time frame for major change in the energy infrastructure has been about fifty years.

The second major issue is energy security, especially as it relates to the supply of oil and natural gas. Not only are there complicated geopolitical issues due to the instability and unpredictability of the Middle East, but there are also geological issues, such as whether oil production is going to peak sometime in the next ten, twenty, or thirty years because of a need to access resources that are more difficult and expensive to produce. If it does, then there will be an exacerbation of some of the security concerns. Furthermore, let me add that the oil and natural gas supplies are by no means the only security concerns associated with energy. There are infrastructure security issues, such as protecting the distribution networks for energy. And yet another problem we face is the possibility of international development of nuclear power leading to nuclear weapons proliferation.

The third major issue is the environmental consequences of energy use. Climate change goes to the very heart of the energy infrastructure because fossil fuels account for 85% of our primary energy use. The problem with fossil fuels is that they produce carbon dioxide. The greenhouse gas mitigation challenge is to control carbon dioxide emissions, while, at least today, still having fossil fuels as the dominant energy source. This is a major paradox and a major concern. If one sets a doubling of pre-industrial carbon dioxide concentrations as a benchmark for entering into a danger zone for climate change, then we will exhaust our carbon dioxide emissions budget in approximately sixty years.

Here at MIT, we are developing technology and policy options that will effectively address these three issues. My colleague John Deutch and I have assembled MIT faculty groups, drawn from all parts of the Institute—there are four different schools taking part—to do

analytically and technically based analysis of different technology pathways. In 2003, we published a report on nuclear power as a possible major contributor to this combination of challenges. We are very close to another one on the future of coal in a greenhouse gas constrained world. At MIT, we can combine strong technically based efforts with our strengths in economics, political science, and the social sciences to really talk about how these issues come together. We hope this research will strongly influence the national and international debates.

What recent changes affect your research today?

Well, I've mentioned these three major drivers, but I would say the issue that has really changed dramatically over the last ten or fifteen years is this focus on climate change and its implications for energy. The need to address climate change is now a serious topic of international discussion. There are differences in approach—our government is suggesting a technology led approach while others favor a policy led approach. But our view is that there won't be a solution without both working together.

Another major change is that industry is now taking the lead in this discussion. Major American international companies are now recognizing that climate change is going to be dealt with in a significant way. Businessmen are practical. They just want to know the rules, and they generally feel that they can make money if they know the rules.

When you consider all of this together, you can see that the landscape is changing dramatically for energy and energy research. I would also like to add that there are other areas of research I and my students are working on. For example, there's a PhD student working on photovoltaics, another student is working on biofuels, and another is working on distributed generation that combines heat and power for very high efficiency. All these pathways, in addition to the large base load activities like nuclear and coal, are very important as well.

You have addressed this to some degree already, but where do you see your work in a global context and where do you see it going?

Well we have indeed covered that to a certain extent. I'll just note that the nuclear power study that we published in 2003 clearly has influenced the international debate about the future of nuclear power. Members of our group have spoken around the world about the results. When MIT pulls together a group of faculty and does an objective, honest, technically and analytically based piece of work, we are well respected. Not everyone agrees with everything we conclude, but there has been a very gratifying interest in understanding where we are coming from and why we reached our conclusions, followed by a very healthy debate.

What are the implications of your work? Are there downsides?

The apparent downsides come precisely from having influenced the debate. For example, we feel that many of the discussions involving nuclear power that are taking place now in government and industry have at least some roots in the dialogue that we helped generate. Some might view that as a downside, because many people would rather see nuclear power phased out. Others complain that we make nuclear power seem too expensive. We consider ourselves neither supporters nor enemies of nuclear power. We view ourselves as supporters of resolving environmental, security, and supply issues. The greenhouse gas problem is so difficult. Frankly, the challenge of meeting greenhouse gas emissions stabilization is severely underestimated in the public debate. Consequently, we do not favor any specific technology. Our view is that if a technology might make a significant contribution to resolving the climate change problem, then we cannot afford to take it off the table, and we should do serious, hard analysis about what would enable it to be part of the solution. That is the spirit. We are just trying to contribute to a responsible solution to this great challenge of our time.

Interviewed 2/21/06

MEG JACOBS

Associate Professor of History

What are you working on here at MIT?

I am writing a book about the energy crisis of the 1970's. I began that project because I am interested in how American politics changed in the late 20th century. Throughout much of the last century, from the Great Depression on, there was the expectation that in a moment of crisis the government would come to the aid and rescue of its citizens. Today, we live in a different political moment where there is much more emphasis on self-reliance and market mechanisms to help citizens through difficult times. I'm interested in that broader shift in world trends that we've seen lately, from the New Deal liberalism of the 1930's to the current influence of the conservative right.

During my research, it became clear to me that the 70's was the critical point of transition in this shift. In both the election of 1968 and landslide re-election in 1972, Richard Nixon ran under the promise of scaling back the reach of government in people's lives. That idea of scaling government back, of government being too intrusive, has grown and been embraced by Republicans and Democrats alike. That is why the energy crisis is a compelling topic. It became a stage upon which politicians and political strategists could act out liberal vs. conservative policy responses to a crisis.

What changes in the recent past have influenced your work?

Well, my first book was called *Pocketbook Politics: Economic Citizenship in 20th Century America*. It is about how American citizens, beginning around 1900, maybe a little bit earlier, came to have expectations that the government owed them something. In other words, that by virtue of being citizens—or in some cases not even citizens, but immigrants or newcomers to the country—the government owed them a high standard of living, or what became known as an American standard of living. That expectation was a move away from the 19th century notion of self-reliance and toward the notion that the government should involve itself in basic issues, like making sure the meat packers don't charge too much for meat.

How is it that citizens began to feel that the government ought to have a stake and responsibility in regulating such basic elements of our lives? That impulse is rooted in

economics, which is why I call it pocketbook politics. Often, we think of marketplace issues and political activism as separate arenas. That is, if you are concerned about your pocketbook, you're not so interested in the community and what would benefit the public. What I found in my research that was quite interesting is that for much of the 20th century, people equated increasing their own riches with benefiting the public good. The idea was that the only way America could become an abundant consumer society was if everyone actually had the capacity to consume. What we saw was the shift away from self-reliance, hard work, strength of character, sobriety, and thriftiness, to this notion that in an industrialized economy, the ups and downs individuals face are not necessarily questions of character, but issues of public policy. In my first book, I wrote about everything from housewives going on strike over the price of meat, to unionized workers going on strike for higher wages. In both instances, there is the expectation that the government should regulate in the public interest and, in so doing, benefit each individual consumer. That was the theme of the book.

A phrase that was used throughout most of the 20th century was "purchasing power"—not just in the technical, economist sense of how much a dollar is worth but, literally, how much money do I have and what will it buy for me. In the decades of the 20's, 30's, 40's, and 50's, we see the emergence and growth of the idea that the federal government should protect an individual's purchasing power. Now, at some moment the expectations of what citizens could rely on their government to do for them changed. That is how I became interested in my second book. I wanted to know how and when that happened. The kinds of things I like to study—as a scholar and historian—are these types of everyday market ideas and how they change the way people think about political obligations and expectations. That is what fascinates me.

Very interesting.

The energy crisis seemed perfect to me because it was real every day. It was essentially the first shared problem since the Great Depression. Over the course of the 1970's, prices at the pump went from 35 cents per gallon to over a dollar. When prices broke the dollar mark, everyone thought the world that they had known was gone forever. People thought this spelled the end of American dominance in the world. The gas line seemed to embody America's dramatic reversal. You had cars, which were the embodiment of post-war boom and prosperity, now lined up and unable to get the gas they needed.

Today, we are in a more conservative moment in which Americans' faith in their government to help them has eroded. I thought that if I looked at this period in the 1970's, I would be able to see that process very clearly already in the works. Surprisingly, that wasn't the case. The world of the 70's—to me—ended up looking more like the world of the 30's than the world of today. That was interesting in terms of political expectations. You had Richard Nixon, who is a Republican, come into office. He's in office when the first oil shock hits, which is the Arab embargo that begins in the fall of 1973 and lasts through the spring of '74. Nixon then suggests Project Independence. This is the idea that America should free itself from its reliance on foreign sources of oil. The way to do that is to boost our own domestic supply, and the way to do that is to basically let businesses do whatever they want.

Ironically, this was right at the peak of environmentalism. Environmentalism was going strong in the late 60's and early 70's. The EPA had just been created and oil production was heavily regulated. The initial solution to the gas shortage, which would be the market solution, was to get rid of all these regulations. The logic was, if we're going to be independent, we need to let the oil companies drill wherever they want. I'm putting this a bit crudely, but you get the point. In fact, what ended up happening was that Americans still very much expected the government to do something. The number one demand was that government should roll back the price of gasoline at the pump. That is hard to imagine today. In February 1974, several months into the embargo, the nation's long-haul truckers—the people who transport fruit, vegetables, produce, meat, consumer products, and household goods—staged a strike. 100,000 truckers went out on strike. Their number one demand was for the government to cut prices at the pump. This is a demand that actually got written into a piece of legislation in Congress. Nixon ultimately vetoed the bill, but that suggests how far things got.

Additionally, there evolved the idea that government should begin a rationing program. Each person would get booklets with coupons redeemable for 35 gallons of gas per month, and everyone would have to make do with that. This plan was championed by the Speaker of the House and the Senate Majority Leader—both Democrats, by the way—as the number one thing to do. In spite of Nixon's electoral success, there still existed this strong expectation that government should provide for its citizens. I didn't think I would find that. There was also the sense that there were clear villains in this story. Of course, the clear villains were the big oil companies. So in public opinion polls, even though this was an embargo from Arab countries, if you asked who was to blame, the answer was big American oil companies. There was widespread feeling that this shortage was completely fabricated and the oil tankers were waiting offshore for prices go higher. That was reported.

One of the fun things I got to do, writing a book on the subject, was to go to the television news archives at Vanderbilt University in Nashville and watch all the old nightly news reports from the 70's about the energy crisis. You can see Walter Cronkite telling the American public that this crisis is contrived and artificial. This sort of anti-corporate flavor is very different from what we experience today. So what does that mean in terms of how I think about today's issues, or how today's issues make me think about those issues?

Yes. That actually brings us to my third question. Can we talk about this in a global context?

The question of running out of gas and the question of polluting the environment are related but different issues. The one thing that was very much on the table in the 70's––and we need to consider again today—was alternative energy sources, both from the point of view of conserving what we have and also not polluting the environment. In the 70's, along with these New Deal style efforts to regulate prices and police corporations, there was also, coming from the Democrats, the push for a major commitment on behalf of the government for alternative energy research. Now, once again, we must have a New Deal for energy because, as you know, alternative energies are expensive and oil companies are not going to invest to do that research without incentive. So the same issues are coming back.

What's interesting is that these projects did not get very far in the 70's. This was a time of perceived crisis, and yet we did not reap any substantial, long-term gains in terms of alternative energy solutions. That's worth thinking about today, especially from the point of view of MIT and how they're going to move forward on their energy initiative. As you know, our president, Susan Hockfield, has made a big commitment to solving the future energy crisis, and MIT, of course, is very well positioned to help in that area. It's just a question of whether they are going to work with industry or government. Will both the political will and necessary capital be there to actually solve the energy crisis, both in terms of the environment and the conservation of resources? Will this be attainable? My job here at MIT really is to say that it's not just about coming up with the right technologies. How we finance them is just as important as developing the political will to implement them. The context is everything.

When I am asked to give talks around campus, I often speak about the politics and difficulties of implementation involved in commitments to new alternative energies. I also talk about public opinion. How willing are Americans to support and pay for new technologies? Some of my colleagues—in political science, for example—do polling. They ask, "If your energy bill goes up five dollars a month but we can have cleaner coal, is that worth it to you?" Then they raise it to ten and fifteen dollars a month and chart the responses.

One terrifically exciting thing about being here at MIT is that the students are fascinated with the problem of global warming. You don't necessarily think of MIT as a political campus, but with the issue of global warming, students get involved. The MIT Energy Club is huge. Students are really very motivated and interested in this problem. It's an exciting time, both because I believe they're smart enough to come up with real solutions, and also because it speaks directly to this generational shift and the evolution of public consciousness and concern over these issues.

Do you think the government has to intervene in order for something to be done about the issues we are facing right now—for example, global warming?

Absolutely.

Do you see possibilities for that in our political system?

You know, it's a good question, and a complicated question, and one I don't pretend to have the answer to. In the 1970's, 83% of the population believed that the fuel crisis was phony and that it had been contrived by big business. That seriously undercut the political will to do anything about it. So the question is how to mobilize public opinion and political will in order to effect change. I am hopeful that global warming is becoming a greater part of the national agenda than it has been in the past. If it resonates in the public sphere, that puts pressure on government to act. We'll see what Al Gore does with his political capital and whether he wants to get back into the race or just address this issue as an elder statesman. It's not enough that everyone in Cambridge sees *An Inconvenient Truth*. That's not going to do it. But you do see that more and more people are aware that global warming is a problem. MIT is perfectly poised—if it does it the right way—to not only do the necessary science to come up with technical solutions, but also use its influence to develop the public momentum this crisis requires.

Is there a downside to your work? Or rather, are there perhaps negative aspects to the process?

The message I peddle around campus when I speak is that change is hard, but not impossible. If you look at the environmental movement, it's a pretty amazing grass-roots story. A major level of public awareness was built up in a rather short period of time. You have the early, seminal consciousness-raising moments, like the publication of Rachel Carson's *Silent Spring* in 1962, and a mere eight years later, 20 million people turn out for the first Earth Day. This created such a high level of public awareness that Richard Nixon, a Republican, signed into being both the creation of the Environmental Protection Agency and the Clean Air Act. That is substantial. So, history provides volumes of cautionary tales, but they are interspersed with moments of true hope. In history, there is no such thing as linear progress. Nixon signed the Clean Air Act, yet rejected the Clean Water Act. It's a push and pull. I don't know if we should necessarily consider that a downside, but it does temper one's optimism regarding the prospects for change.

On a personal level, I love my job. I love being at MIT because it is such a vibrant intellectual culture. Education and understanding are the elements that precipitate change. Right now, I'm getting attention because I'm writing a book about the energy crisis. People come to me because, based on my knowledge of what has occurred in the past, they imagine I might have insights as to what we should do now. History is not so clear-cut. The only thing policy history shows us is the complexity of political change. It's quite a useful dialogue and exchange, but not necessarily the window to a solution.

Interviewed 5/1/07

DAN COHN

Senior Research Scientist in the Laboratory for Energy and the Environment and the Plasma Science and Fusion Center
Head of the Plasma Technology Division of the Plasma Science and Fusion Center

What are you working on here at MIT?

My interest has been in the energy area. Most recently, I've been working on ways to make cars more efficient while still being stringent on air pollution regulations and also trying to minimize the cost of improving fuel economy. The goal is to make fuel-efficient cars that are economically attractive to people—that is, cars that people would want to buy because there is an economic benefit. In this way, my colleagues and I feel that technology really has an impact. We want to see vehicles such as these in wide use so that there will be a significant overall reduction of oil consumption and green house gas emission.

Leslie Bromberg, John Heywood, and I have been working for some time, in different ways, to make engines more efficient. Lately, we've been working on a concept we call the Ethanol Turbo Boosted Gasoline Engine. The idea here is to use a very small amount of ethanol to enable a very significant increase in fuel efficiency of a gasoline engine at very low cost. Injecting the ethanol directly into the cylinder enables much higher performance. It allows you to get a lot more power out of a small, high-efficiency engine and therefore replace a larger engine. Through this replacement, we believe that the fuel efficiency gain will be close to that obtained by a hybrid vehicle, but at a far lower cost.

One of the reasons the gasoline hybrid enjoys a significant increase in efficiency is because it uses a small engine most of the time, and when more power is needed, it uses the electric motor with the stored electricity from the battery. What we're doing with our highly turbocharged engine is analogous to the hybrid in that we also have a very small engine most of the time, but when we need the high power we use very aggressive turbocharging, and we actually think it's a more effective system than storing energy in a battery. Also, in contrast to a hybrid, where the weight of the vehicle is actually increased because of the weight of the battery and all the extra equipment, here the weight of the vehicle would be reduced. This is because we're taking a big engine, like the V8, and replacing it with a four-cylinder engine, which is much smaller, has a lot of turbocharging, and a high compression ratio. Again, we get a lot more power out of the small size engine while operating it much more efficiently. So, that's one of my major interests right now.

We wanted to get this out into the world quickly, so John, Leslie and I formed a company which we call Ethanol Boosting Systems. We're now in the process of developing that technology for commercial use. To accomplish this, we formed a research and development collaboration with the Ford Motor Company. They recently obtained engine test results, consistent with our predictions, which show that this can be a way to rather significantly increase the amount of power in a given size engine.

What is the time frame in which this might be implemented?

Well if everything goes to plan, these engines can go into production in 2012. Our goal is to get something out there. Because of its low extra cost, and because of its small departure from existing technology, it could be rapidly deployed in a way that would really make a difference. As you know, reducing our oil consumption is a critical energy need, and improving the transportation sector, particularly vehicles that consume gasoline, is vital.

Considering the urgency of global warming, do you see this as a transition technology or a car of the future?

I think it can be both. It certainly is a transition technology because it allows us to use the internal combustion engine more efficiently and uses a renewable fuel, ethanol, in an economically attractive way. So, because everything happens so slowly in the automobile industry, I could see that this would be a technology that would be of great use for at least a few decades. In the longer term, we might see improvements in the production and availability of ethanol, it may be economically more attractive, or gasoline may become more expensive. Therefore, the relative appeal of ethanol versus gasoline may change to the point where more ethanol can and will be used. As far as other technologies are concerned, there has been a lot of interest in fuel cells, for instance. My sense though is that it will be many decades before that technology becomes practical and economically attractive. I think for many years to come, it will be very hard for other engine systems to compete with internal combustion engine based technology. So for some time, we will have vehicles that largely run on gasoline, and we can use ethanol to make them more efficient.

Would you like to discuss other aspects of your work?

Let me tell you what my orientation has been. I have tried to develop new, environmentally friendly energy technologies that can get out and have an impact as soon as possible. A separate area that I've worked in, along those lines, has been new technology to improve the handling of waste and to use it as a source for clean energy and clean fuels.

In this technology, we make use of a plasma—an electrically conducting gas which looks like a scaled down bolt of lightning—as a means to process waste in a way that's much more environmentally attractive than incineration or landfilling. The science and applications of plasmas is what this lab, the Plasma Science and Fusion Center, is all about. The main emphasis has been on the investigation of very hot plasmas as a means to produce energy from fusion, the energy source of the stars and the sun. In the early 1990's, we investigated the use of plasmas for waste processing as a short-term application that complements the longer-term pursuit of fusion energy. Initially, we built a large plasma furnace here in the lab to show that this basic approach made sense. After this project was completed, we spun off a company. It is located out in Richland, Washington near the DOE (Department of Energy) Hanford site. The company—Integrated Environmental Technologies, LLC (IET)—is now providing a new type of plasma based furnace for commercial use. This type of furnace, which we call a plasma enhanced melter, can process a variety of wastes—medical waste, chemical waste, nuclear waste—in an environmentally protective and economically attractive manner. Looking toward the future with this technology, we see it as a very good way to take all types of wastes—for example, municipal waste—and turn them into clean electricity or liquid transportation fuels. So, the orientation is to develop near-term technologies that have near-term impacts on the areas of energy and the environment.

So, the toxicity of these different things that need to be disposed of is dealt with in a different way? What happens to the toxins?

The waste material has an organic component and an inorganic component. The organic component is heated at very high temperature, the complex molecules are broken up, the carbon and hydrogen are reformed into what's called the hydrogen-rich gas—it's a very good gas for producing electricity or for making fuels—and the hazardous materials are separated so they are trapped before they exit.

I see, so they are not going into the environment.

Undesirable emissions are suppressed to such a low level that they are virtually eliminated. In fact, you can imagine an essentially closed cycle, where in comes the waste and out comes the clean stream of hydrogen synthesis gas. The plasma furnace converts the waste into an environmentally benign and useful product. That's the organic part of the waste. The inorganic part—metals and glass—is actually melted into a form that is also benign. Instead of being in the form of ash, which is a byproduct of incinerators and can be hazardous, the waste is in the form of black glass. It actually looks like lava from a volcano. Glass is an extremely stable form of matter.

Do you want to touch on any other fields?

Well, yes, I think it would be useful to discuss one other technology, which we developed at the Plasma Science and Fusion Center, called plasmatron reformer technology. This is a small device that reforms—that is, converts—diesel fuel or gasoline into hydrogen-rich gas. It is used to enable effective emissions control for diesel vehicles. Diesel engines are very efficient. That's why they are favored among trucks and buses. However, they have a much higher pollutant emission level than gasoline engines, and there is a strong need to reduce these emissions. EPA regulations actually require large future reductions. Our technology, which is a plasmatron reformer enhanced exhaust treatment system, is a promising candidate for addressing this need. To develop this technology, we teamed with ArvinMeritor, a major U.S. truck components manufacturer. They used the plasmatron technology, together with a new type of exhaust treatment catalyst, in a prototype diesel bus which they drove around their test track in the Midwest. This vehicular test successfully showed that the emissions can be quite substantially reduced. We hope that this is another near-term technology that could have a significant beneficial impact on the environment.

In the recent past, what changes in and around your field have most affected your research?

Certainly, using energy more efficiently has become increasingly important. People are aware of the potential threat of generating excess CO_2 and its connection to global warming. The concerns about this have been increased over the past several years, as have concerns about oil security. Additionally, with regard to oil, the high prices, the potential problems caused by the tight balance between supply and demand, and the potential for large price spikes and disruptions are greater than, say, few years ago. So, it's clear that it has become very important to develop more efficient, near-term methods to propel cars and trucks. Another thing that happened is related to the increased importance of developing alternative fuels, such as ethanol. Of course, that relates to a variety of things that I've just talked about. And finally, in the environmental area, the fact that more countries are industrializing, points to the importance of providing better ways to deal with various wastes. It's a significant problem here and it's an even greater problem in rapidly developing countries like China. The industrial advances in these countries have made the development of practical technologies in this area more urgent.

Where do you see your work in a global context and what is your vision for the future? We've talked about this a bit, but maybe you want to take it further.

Well, in the case of the Ethanol Turbo Boosted Gasoline Engine, my vision for the future is that it will be a technology that will be economically attractive and, once put in production, will be rapidly accepted and deployed worldwide. We hope that widespread use of this technology could lead to the reduction of U.S. oil consumption by 1.5 to 2 million barrels per day. In the initial form, it could reduce gasoline consumption of a typical vehicle by 20% to 25%, and that's almost completely a result of efficiency gain, not the increased use of ethanol. This technology would also make ethanol more economically attractive. We will then see a further reduction as the engine concept becomes more efficient over time. We see this as potentially having an important impact in the next few decades in reducing oil consumption and green house gas production.

With regard to the waste treatment, the plasma enhanced melter is a technology that I'd like to see become the norm, rather than throwing waste on the ground and landfilling it. The present approach has the potential to harm the water supply, the soil, and the air. Furthermore, there is no reutilizing of value in resources that are discarded. The plasma enhanced melter technology is also highly preferable to incineration, which is problematic due to undesirable air emissions and potentially harmful ash. We see this as our goal for the future and the new standard for dealing with waste. We want to be environmentally protective and optimize recyclable materials. That's my hope for the future.

What are the implications of your work? Are there downsides?

I have to say that I don't see any real downsides. I think the challenge is to make these technologies economically attractive. I believe that is absolutely essential in order to have a big impact. And I believe that it's doable, but we have to work hard at it.

DAN COHN

Do you think we should be doing more? Do you think this is enough to avert global warming? We are experiencing major climate change.

I'm glad you're asking this question. With regard to climate change, if in fact it is as serious as some of the projections indicate—and we certainly need to take out insurance against that possibility—then the work I mentioned could be a significant step toward a solution. Of course, a number of other steps are needed as well. There has to be work done across the board. We need ways to make coal cleaner and to sequester CO_2 emissions. In short, we need better ways to produce electric power. My own view is that eventually nuclear power will have to play a greater role. Unfortunately, there are major questions of how to deal with its inherent economic, environmental, and weapons proliferation issues. We will have challenges, but I think these are challenges that can be met.

With regard to waste, developing technologies to dispose and recycle more efficiently is important. But I think it's also important for people to consume less. Technology can't provide the total solution, but it is a very important part of it and is an area where people at MIT could make a significant contribution.

Interviewed 9/11/06

JOHN G. KASSAKIAN

Professor of Electrical Engineering and Computer Science
Director of the Laboratory for Electromagnetic and Electronic Systems

What are you working on here at MIT?

My field is power electronics, which is the use of electronics to control electric energy. The contexts are pretty varied. Two of the biggest are electric energy storage and transportation. We've had a very large program in automotive electronics and electrical systems where we have proposed, and have had accepted, a new 42 volt standard for voltage in cars. This was a very significant accomplishment because it's hard to get the auto industry to agree on something that radical. Unfortunately, the implementation has been significantly delayed because of the auto industry's economic problems at the moment, especially in the U.S.

But there are two other research programs that I think are very significant. One is the development of what we call a nanotube-based ultracapacitor. This is a device that functions like a battery, but is fundamentally different in that there is no electrochemical process that involves mass transport. It is strictly the storage of ions like you have in a capacitor. If we are successful, this device could replace batteries in all sorts of applications, with a much higher energy density, a much higher power density and, essentially, infinite life. Hopefully, it will be at a cost that is reasonable.

What are some of the applications for this ultracapacitor?

Any place where you use a battery—hybrid cars, for example. Your camera probably uses a lithium ion battery. If, instead, you had an ultracapacitor that had the same energy density, you'd be able to charge it in about three minutes rather than half an hour or an hour.

You said you're trying to change the standards in the auto industry, and you actually did affect change. Could you specify the advantages?

The problem for the auto industry is that there is so much electrical equipment in modern cars that a 12-volt battery, which is the standard today, has a very difficult time supporting it all. This changeover process to a new voltage was actually started by Mercedes Benz. They were under pressure to continue to increase the electrical components in their cars

and they realized the need for higher voltage. In order to determine a higher voltage, they first needed the rest of the industry to agree on it. So, they set a standard. Your car today has at least a dozen computers and everything is operated electrically. You've got electric windows, electric antilock brakes, electric throttle, radio, CD player, navigation system, televisions, and so on. Huge amounts of electric energy are used.

Now, the ultracapacitor is designed to take advantage of the new materials that have been developed using carbon nanotubes. These are very small diameter, very long tubes of single sheets of carbon and they have very low resistivity. They are extremely small and you can grow them as sort of a forest on a conducting substrate, which is then used as one of the plates in this capacitor, and you use another one as the other plate. The idea is that with this very large surface area that becomes available, you can get very high capacitance values. So you can store a lot of energy.

The other project, which is the thermophotovoltaic conversion of electricity, relates again to the automotive, or transportation, industry but also has applications elsewhere. Very simply stated, this is the use of solar cells, except you're not using the solar radiation to impinge on these cells. Instead, you're burning a fuel in an emitter that glows, and it's the light from this emitter that is captured by these photocells and converted to electricity. So, this is a device that can create a flame and convert it into electricity using these photocells.

The idea is to use this in an automobile, or in a truck, to generate the electricity necessary. This is a better solution than a generator, which is what we use now. In order for the generator to be operating, your engine has to be running. For fuel economy purposes, one of the modes of future driving is that engines will shut off when a car is not in motion. If you come to a stoplight, your engine shuts off. If you come to a traffic jam, your engine shuts off. In the meantime, you don't want to lose the electricity in the car, so this is one way of continuing to provide that electricity while your engine is off.

There are two things that are exciting about this. First of all, it's not a new idea. It's an old idea that's been around since the late 50's. But the materials for building the photocells and the materials for actually controlling the spectrum of the light haven't been available. Today, through photonics and the development of compound semiconducting materials, we are able to create a spectrum that illuminates the photocell in a way that is more matched to the characteristics of the cell. The second exciting thing is that when you have the fuel burning in the emitter creating light, you also have some heat that's left over. We propose to use that heat in what's known as an absorption cycle air conditioning system. Years ago, these refrigeration systems were more common. People had refrigerators that ran on gas, not electricity. So, again, it's an old technology. But take, for example, one of these large tractor-trailers that is parked at night somewhere with the driver sleeping in the cab. What he does today is he leaves his engine running, or uses an auxiliary generator, to keep the cab cool, run his television, and everything else. With the absorption cycle air conditioning system, you could provide the air conditioning and the electricity more efficiently, it would not make any noise, and it would meet the emission requirements that are coming down the pike for truckers. For example, they're not going to be able to just let their rigs idle by the side of the road anymore.

So, those are two examples of what I think are research programs that are addressing two really critical needs: one is in transportation and the other—which is a huge need—is in energy storage.

What recent changes in or around your field affect your research today? You've already mentioned technological aspects, but how has public policy affected it?

Certainly this business with the truckers is public policy, emissions is public policy, and energy efficiency is public policy. My field has been greatly influenced by public policy because of the demands for energy efficiency, and power electronics is one of the ways of gaining efficiency. Efficiency in motors is important because they are everywhere you look. In your home, you have a dozen motors you probably don't even know about. Using electronics to control these motors improves their efficiency quite substantially. Power supplies for even simple things, like a battery charger, now benefit from power electronics because the chargers are much more efficient than they were ten years ago. Power supplies for computers are also much more efficient. The need to keep computers running even during power outages requires power electronics. So all of these things have had a major impact on my particular field.

Energy is a major concern. It's always been a concern, but every once in awhile the spotlight shines on it. Back in the 70's, the spotlight shone on it very brightly, then it kind of dimmed, and now it's back again very brightly. We're concerned about the security of the electric transmission grid and we're concerned about the capacity of the electric transmission generation system. Behind you there, on the floor, that black thing is a piece of a 345,000 volt underground transmission line that's being used for transmitting electric power to someplace where it will be stepped down. At that voltage level, that's relatively untested technology. The material that is used as the insulator in there is known as crosslink polyethylene. This is being installed in southwest Connecticut in the longest run ever in the world. There's going to be nineteen miles of it. That doesn't sound very long, but for something like this it is quite long.

There are a lot of new developments in the field of energy that are very exciting. Looking to the future, I have no doubt that, sooner or later, society is going to accept nuclear energy as its primary source of electricity. It may not be in our lifetime because there is an awful lot of objection to it. But the fact is that it is the cleanest form of energy, it's not one that we depend upon the rest of the world for, and you don't kill miners of uranium the way we keep killing coal miners.

So you favor a transition to nuclear energy as our main source of energy? What about safety?

Absolutely, that's an issue. There's no question. What happened with Chernobyl was a real disaster of the first order, both for the people there and for the nuclear industry. There was absolutely no excuse for that. The way that reactor was built, it was basically designed to have a failure like this. There is no reactor in any other part of the world that would fail in this way. There was no containment. It was just awful. And of course, it set back the nuclear industry for a long time.

Where do you see your work in a global context and where do you see it going?

I think in the car industry you're going to see more hybrid vehicles and much more electrification of functions in vehicles, even more than you have today. All of that involves electromechanics and electronics, power electronics. This energy storage business is going to be a really big one. If we're successful with those two projects I described, they're both going to make major impacts on how we use energy—especially the capacitors. Energy storage is a huge problem today. It is unlike almost anything else. It is unlike oil. It is unlike grain. In fact, it's the big problem that we face with deregulated electricity markets. You can't store energy. You can buy futures in it, but unlike futures in oranges or wheat, or bacon, or hog bellies, you can't store it. This has created a big challenge for those who are dealing with it.

Are you more inclined to help existing markets or do you feel that we should also make major changes and adjustments in terms of driving, designing our cities, and using energy?

I think it would be great if people changed their habits, but they're not going to. There are several different ways of looking at that problem. First of all, it's hard to envision how you would change habits without changing lifestyle and standards of living. Infrastructure is a big issue. We're a suburban country. Yes we've got big cities, but people commute into the cities. Transportation is a major factor in our economy because that is how people get to work. Look at what's happened to air travel. Even with the hassle of air travel today, people are still flying. The airplanes are full. It's a bigger hassle today than it ever was in the past, but people still feel they have to travel for business purposes. There are a lot of other business technologies that are available—WebEx, video conferencing, audio conferencing—but face time is still a priority. Are people going to turn down their thermostats to 65 degrees in the winter? I don't think so. Are people going to stop air conditioning their houses in the summer? I don't think so. Are people going to stop driving? Not at today's gasoline prices, not even at three or four dollars a gallon. There's been no change. To answer your question, I think it would be nice if there was some way of changing habits that responded to the present needs, but I'm unsure about that ever happening.

What are the implications of your work? Is there a downside?

Of course not, there's no downside. All of this work that I've described has basically been directed towards making better use of electric energy. Electric energy is the highest quality form of energy we have. When we speak of quality, we talk about what it is capable of doing. Electricity is by far the most flexible of any current form of energy. Getting the electricity is the process where we have all our difficulties—emissions, efficiency, and so forth. Through these programs, we are trying to address some of the associated issues. The downside is if we don't succeed.

Interviewed 10/5/06

MUJID KAZIMI

Professor of Mechanical Engineering
Director of the Center for Advanced Nuclear Energy Systems

What are you working on here at MIT?

Our work focuses on improving nuclear power technology options for the future. The key element is the fuel. It must be designed in such a way that the plant, which is built around the fuel, can be efficient—both in terms of housing and cooling the fuel, and also in converting into electricity the thermal power that is produced by the nuclear fission process.   To that end, we're developing fuel that can handle a higher power density than is possible in today''s fuel. Therefore, it will require less volume to produce the amount of power we need, which, in turn, will lower cost.

We also have new power conversion systems that are more efficient and thus can reduce the amount of material that is needed to produce a certain amount of electricity. And looking forward, we must find solutions for handling the discharged fuel. Today, discharged fuel is stored at the nuclear power plants. The plan is for it to go into a deep depository currently proposed in Nevada, but which hasn't yet been licensed. We are also working on understanding the options for recycling fuel, as 95% of it is potentially useful in that capacity.

So, there are three main focus areas: more power per unit volume in the reactor, a more compact energy conversion system, and an optimum method for recycling the useful parts of the spent fuel. At the same time though, we must at least maintain all the current safety characteristics, if not improve upon them.

What could the recycled fuel be used for?

It could be used for future energy generation in similar reactors. Of course, it has to be separated from the waste and remanufactured in the right proportions.

How do you go about your research?

In the first two of the three areas I just mentioned, we do tests. As far as recycling is concerned, that's a bit more complicated. We don't perform tests here, but we do provide ideas which will hopefully be tested at national laboratories that have more

capabilities.

For fuel design, we start by picking a desirable new fuel geometry. We also analyze the performance of the fuel in the core. We can estimate what sort of arrangement would make sense from a neutron balance point of view and from a thermal cooling point of view. All of that is done by computer codes created around certain principles. Then we ask ourselves what we need to know in order to make our calculations more certain. In some cases, it is a question of whether we can manufacture a particular fuel in, perhaps, non-traditional geometry.

With conversion systems, we first analyze what we want based on the physics involved and the engineering that is possible. Once we get to a configuration we like, we ask ourselves what is uncertain about it. For example, one thing that goes into this conversion cycle is a heat exchanger. A heat exchanger is necessary, especially one that is compact. However, the manufacturing of compact heat exchangers is a relatively new industrial activity. There are ready-made heat exchangers, but we want to improve them.

What recent changes in and around your field have affected your research?

The growing concern about the environmental effects of fossil fuels has been a big change. Obviously, the U.S. and the world use mostly fossil fuels for electricity, as well as for transportation, and people are much more concerned today about CO_2 emissions than in times past. That has paved the way for nuclear energy to reemerge as a more environmentally acceptable alternative. Based on everything I have read, I think there is a definite correlation between CO_2 emissions and the warming of the earth. The exact amount and rate may be uncertain, but the trend is not uncertain. We must do something about it now because it will soon be too late.

The other thing that is very important is the fact that for more than 25 years now, we've had hundreds of nuclear power plants operating in the United States without any accidents that have harmed the public. Initially, people were worried about the safety of nuclear power plants. We did have several dangerous events—particularly Three Mile Island, in which the entire core was destroyed. Although no harmful radioactivity was released outside the containment area, it was a significant malfunction. Subsequently, public acceptance of nuclear power reached its nadir. Since that time, many safety modifications have been added to better defend against accidents. The lessons of the first 25 years in the history of nuclear power have made it possible for the second 25 years to be much more safe and reliable. These power plants are operating, on average, over 90% of the time. They need to shut down every 18 or 24 months to refuel, but the incidences of shutdown due to other reasons have significantly decreased. That means that they are being managed reasonably well, which adds to the public confidence and promotes the idea that future plants will be built to operate safely.

We have also seen technologically based benefits. Nuclear power plants are big-ticket items. They are multi-billion dollar investments and cannot be changed much once they are built. However, advances in computational abilities have allowed us to process information faster, create more efficient simulations, and apply remedial actions better. We also have a better understanding of material flaws. Many problems arise due to degradation of materials, which is a result of either high temperature or the radiation field. We now understand more about how to combat this degradation of materials, how to detect flaws ahead of time by applying nondestructive evaluations better, and how to make the right replacements and perform the right maintenance before problems arise.

Where do you see your work in a global context? Where do you see it going?

Up until about 1998, we were much more focused on how to improve the reliability and safety of existing power plants. However, we now need to look ahead to innovative ideas for the future. That's why we've organized the Center for Advanced Nuclear Systems. We were probably the first center worldwide to actually concentrate on advanced technologies for future reactors—things like alternative coolants and alternative emissions. Our current focus is to examine new ideas that can improve the reliability and economic viability of nuclear power, and also expand the applications wider than just electricity. I think there will be an opportunity in the next 20 to 25 years to link nuclear energy to the transportation industry. Electricity may also eventually become a more important part of the transportation sector. Right now, in the near-term, this would come more in the form of applying heat in order to make the heavy oils more fluid and more easily transportable, or applying hydrogen to increase their usability for burning. I think globally, and others are beginning to do so as well. For example, two years ago, the Tokyo Institute of Technology formed a center of excellence for innovative nuclear technology. I believe we will see more and more activities at universities seeking to achieve similar goals.

Do you see nuclear power as a transitional energy source or one that is here to stay?

I see nuclear energy as one of a number of energies the world will need. Unlike fossil sources, it doesn't produce harmful emissions in the form of carbon dioxide. Unlike renewable energy, it is a high-density, concentrated source of power and doesn't require the vast amounts of land that are required for the production of energy from solar or wind. Furthermore, not every part of the world is suitable for those renewable sources. Some places are blessed with having a lot of hydropower or solar reception throughout the year. Some are not. Wind blows differently in different parts of the world.

I do think we will need a backup for our current system, and I think that future growth will be in nuclear and renewables. We will see continued use of fossils, because oil and gas are, at the moment, easier to transport and apply. Also, coal is rather abundant in important high demand places like the United States and China. Because it is in abundance, it will be used. For the last 15 years or so, nuclear energy has accounted for roughly 7% of the total energy production in the world. I expect that will grow. I would be comfortable if that number grew to about 25%.

Why not more?

There are certain issues inherent to the use of nuclear energy that require resolution. For example, because it is such a sophisticated technology, it is not possible to expect that all countries and communities will be able to assume the necessary maintenance, inspections, and general security procedures. Furthermore, nuclear fuel could be diverted for use in weaponry. So, there will be some limits on the use of that technology, whether it's at the front end, i.e. enrichment, or at the back end, i.e. reprocessing.

I think the world will come up with a system where there would be a certain collaboration—perhaps regional, possibly international—in order to keep the strategic materials out of the hands of untrustworthy groups. It would be natural to use a system where there is redundancy—that is, more than one fuel. We certainly don't want to ever lose a large fraction of the overall energy supply. If you look at today's energy production, oil, gas, and coal are providing perhaps 80% of the energy. Then you have hydro, nuclear, and biomass—mostly wood— providing the remainder. The other renewables have not grown enough to account for a significant percentage.

Regarding possible nuclear proliferation dangers, is the problem at the beginning of the creation cycle, or is it later with whatever materials remain?

This has been a matter of worry from day one. The nuclear era began with the development of weaponry. But its potential benefits to humanity were so compelling that the United States—beginning with the Eisenhower era *Atoms for Peace* program in the late 50's—led the way in the sharing of this technology. The question has always been how much nuclear know-how can we permit in the commercial world without abetting widespread weapons development. This tension continues to this day. The trend has been, essentially, to ask for all countries to promise not to produce weapons, sign the Nuclear Non-Proliferation Treaty, and allow the Intelligent Energy Executive Agency to inspect the plants in order to guarantee peaceful applications. I think we will need an international organization that will provide the fuel initially, and perhaps another organization that takes it at the end.

Can you discuss some design innovations?

There are ideas for making the plants operate for a very long time before needing refueling. Using today's water technology, it is feasible to extend the uninterrupted operation of a plant to maybe 15 years. Using fast reactors, you can go even further. The idea is to keep the structure reasonably small. This way, at the end of the lifetime, you can take away the whole reactor and send in a new one. Therefore, the fuel will never be out of the boxes. Many countries are now working on what we call small or medium reactors. But in the final analysis, when you look at the market and what people have been buying, we haven't seen a big demand for such smaller units, or ones that operate for unusually long times. The Russians have built a small reactor in the neighborhood of 200 megawatts that can be shipped anywhere on a barge. But, I look around the rest of the world and I see many more orders for, and interest in, the large units which require more frequent refueling. If we can find a way to make the long cycle buttoned-up reactors less costly, maybe demand will increase.

Are they safer, in terms of prevention of terrorism?

I do not think there is a difference. The long cycle reactors require higher concentration of the fissionable isotopes at the beginning, but the material is still well bound to the other uranium isotopes. In the reactor, the fuel becomes very radioactive either way. Anybody who gets close to nuclear fuel is going to suffer quite a dose of radiation. Theoretically, you could say that it is safer if it is never outside the vessel. Nuclear fuel, once irradiated, is very difficult to handle. You need sophisticated techniques for remote replacement and transportation. It's not an easy thing to steal.

What are the implications of your work? Is there a downside to this research?

I'm not sure how to answer that. Even if a technology has advantages—say, in safety or waste reduction—it will not be embraced in the market unless it is also economically attractive. This raises the interesting question of whether to simplify advances so the economics will work out better. Very often, you find that it is possible to improve reliability or safety, but if you increase costs, the technology will not be applied. That's why it's always a challenge to improve economics and functionality simultaneously.

I do not think wider use of nuclear energy has more of a downside than other types of energy. Carbon emissions have a downside that's well identified. It is less obvious in the case of renewables. But look at the case of the wind farm in Cape Cod. That has stirred passions because people don't want their views obstructed. There are aesthetic questions when it comes to land use. If we want to supply a big city like Boston with the same amount of electricity it currently uses, do we need to block the land between Route 128 and Interstate 495 just to put the solar plates there?

Being prudent about the use of energy is good. Having multiple resources so we are not surprised in the future by unanticipated downsides is good. And, we must continuously examine ways to improve operating conditions. Right now, from one kilogram of fuel, we produce about 50 megawatt-days of energy, or 1200 megawatt-hours. If we get to 100 megawatt-days per kilogram, we will significantly reduce the amount of space needed for spent fuel storage, by a factor of two. That's an advantage. However, in the process, you're going to be subjecting the materials to more damage because they will be withstanding a higher number of neutrons. There is always some challenge to be faced.

Regarding inherent dangers, the U.S. has never allowed a weak reactor containment building, even from the beginning. Our containment requirements are much more stringent than the requirements that precipitated the Chernobyl accident. But since that time, new developments have added to the defenses—both in the fuel inside the core and in the containment building. In some designs, it is now possible to depend only on natural convection of air to keep things cool and safe. I look at it like the airline business. Safety has improved because they've learned how to inspect, design, and manage better. Though an accident is a possibility, it is neither a likelihood nor an eventuality. The same goes for nuclear energy.

Interviewed 12/6/06

NOAM CHOMSKY

Institute Professor
Professor of Linguistics, Linguistic Theory, Syntax, Semantics, Philosophy of Language

What are you working on here at MIT, or in general?

My work is kind of schizophrenic. I have a professional commitment to linguistics, philosophy, cognitive science, and, as far as understanding the nature of the human mind is concerned, biology. A totally separate track, which is essentially extracurricular, with nothing much to do with being at MIT, is a concern with social and political issues, international affairs, international crises, literal threats to survival, and so on. Actually, I did teach courses on these topics at MIT for about twenty-five years, but on my own time. They weren't part of any curriculum. I may do it here, but it's not MIT's affair.

In matters such as these, there are many choices one can make about what should be high on the agenda, but there are several topics that I think cannot be ignored because they are literally questions of human survival. One of them is suggested by that gentleman over there (points to poster), Bertrand Russell. In 1955, he and Einstein published an appeal in which they called on the people of the world to face a choice that is stark and unavoidable and inevitable: either mankind will end war or the species will be destroyed. They were speaking about nuclear weapons. That threat is greater now than it was when they spoke. Of course, people haven't abandoned war, far from it. In fact, right now our own country reserves, to itself, the right to attack anyone it wants at will, on the basis of an alleged potential threat which doesn't even have to be imminent. It's probably the most extreme position that any state has taken in quite a long time. There is a very serious and growing threat of nuclear war, perhaps even accidental war. The threats are increasing and they're being enhanced by policies of aggressive militarism that are driving other potential targets to respond in comparable ways. All of that leads to what Robert McNamara recently called, "apocalypse soon." There is a fair consensus among strategic analysts that this is a threat that is severe and growing, and it's a threat to survival. In fact, it is the most severe threat to survival. The only comparable threat is environmental disaster, which will sooner or later come in some form or another. One can debate the details, but, again, there is simply an overwhelming consensus among scientists—and it's rare that we find consensus on any topic—that this problem too is severe and growing.

In the case of nuclear war, it is quite clear how to end the crisis. The non-proliferation treaty of 1970 is a bargain, and it's very much in the news right now, but the focus is on

the wrong part. There is one article, Article 4, which says non-nuclear states have the right to enrich uranium for nuclear energy. That's the part that is the focus of attention, and rightfully so. It's a serious issue. But there's a much more serious commitment on the part of the nuclear states, stated in Article 6, to undertake good-faith efforts to eliminate nuclear weapons. That is, in fact, a binding legal obligation determined by the world court about a decade ago. Well, none of the nuclear states have lived up to it, but the United States is well in the lead in violating it. In fact, last May, at the last regular five-year review, the U.S. announced that it is not bound by that obligation. It is, furthermore, developing new nuclear weapons, and there are even veiled threats to use them. So that's the reason why the review collapsed last May, leading to much dismay among arms control specialists.

Additionally, against almost unanimous global opposition, the U.S. is moving on to the militarization of space. Almost 95% of the expenditures in that area are from the United States. That's an extremely serious threat because, again, potential targets will react. Environmental catastrophes are a more long-term threat. But the fewer steps we take now to mitigate it, the worse it will be when it comes. These are two major crises that simply cannot be ignored.

The third crisis is that our own government is enhancing both of those threats. I stress the word government, because the population is opposed. For example, on the environmental issues, you read in the press that the United States was one of the few industrial states that refused to accept the Kyoto Protocols. That is true only if the United States excludes its population. The government refused, but the population is strongly in support of it. In fact, so strongly in support of it that the majority of Bush voters thought that he was in support of it, because it's such an obvious thing to do.

So that leads to a fourth crisis, which is a growing divide, a chasm, between public policy and public opinion. And that is true on a host of issues. In fact, according to very extensive public opinion studies, which are rarely reported, both political parties are well to the right of the general population on quite a wide series of very significant issues, both international and domestic. Well, this fourth crisis yields what is called a democratic deficit. That is, formal, but not seriously functioning, democratic institutions. Now the fourth crisis is, in a sense, the core of all of them. If that can be overcome, if public policy could be brought into conformity with public attitudes, the situation would be considerably improved. It wouldn't end the other crises, but it would lead us a step closer to ending them, especially toward ending the third one, namely that the U.S. is enhancing the dangers. And it could lead toward implementing the means to end the threat of nuclear war and also mitigating the coming environmental catastrophe.

Regarding nuclear war, there are other issues, which are only discussed in the technical literature, which ought to be on the public agenda. There will be fissile materials produced for nuclear energy. The question is, who should produce them? Well, if individual states produce them with contemporary technology, enriching uranium for nuclear energy leads you just a step away from nuclear weapons. So the Bush administration is, in fact, correct in saying that Article 4 of the non-proliferation treaty should be tightened. It was okay in 1970, but it's not okay today. But that means that fissile materials have to be produced under international supervision, with states that want to use them for nuclear energy going to the international agency and, if they can show that it is for peaceful uses, obtaining the right to use them. That's a sensible proposal. Actually, that proposal has been on the table for some years. It was proposed by the head of the International Atomic Energy Agency, Mohamed ElBaradei. But that proposal is dead in the water. The U.S. would never accept that restriction on its unique right to violate international law and treaties. This unique position, by the way, is sometimes called an outlaw state. As far as I'm aware, there is only one state that has accepted that proposal. Iran, in February, said that it would agree to terminate all uranium enrichment if in fact some proposal like Mohamed ElBaradei's was accepted. As far as I'm aware, that wasn't reported, but it is significant. That proposal would be a step towards capping the production of fissile materials.

In 1993, there was a UN resolution calling for a fissile material cutoff treaty to cap production of nuclear weapons and materials. The U.S. is opposed to that. It—the Bush administration particularly—said it wouldn't sign a verifiable cutoff treaty. Nevertheless, the UN disarmament commission did proceed to vote on it. The vote was held in November 2004 and the tally was 147 to 1. There were two abstentions. One was Israel, which reflects that they have to vote with the United States. The second, and much more interesting abstention, was Britain. At the UN session, the British ambassador explained that Britain supported the treaty, but could not vote for it because it was dividing the international community. Namely, dividing it 147 to 1. That tells you something about Britain and its priorities. You have human survival on one side and making sure you don't offend the master on the other side. Well, that wasn't reported either. So we're back to the democratic deficit. I think if people knew about these things, they would say that it is probably the most important vote that's ever been taken at the United Nations and that it is the core of bringing to an end the constant threat of nuclear destruction, which is in fact mounting.

There are ways to proceed and they're not utopian or idealistic or unimaginable, but they require public education, they require the functioning of democratic institutions, and they require the abandonment of the stance that we must be an outlaw state not subject to international law. Similar things can be said about the second major crisis, environmental catastrophe. There are things that can be done. It may be too late to really overcome the crisis, but it can certainly be reduced and mitigated, and steps simply have to be taken at this point by anyone who cares about the world in which their grandchildren are going to live.

In my opinion, these are all core issues and I've spent most of my life, outside of my professional work, addressing them. I write books, I constantly give talks and interviews, and I'm involved with activist groups that are going to do something about it.

Your work is clear. What can we do?

The same thing. There is nothing special about me. It's well known how to bring about changes. We have a unique legacy of freedom and privilege. It was never given as a gift. It was won by popular struggle. We have a basis for proceeding which is better than it ever was in the past. The question is, do we want to use the legacy or abandon it? But there are no major secrets. In the last thirty or forty years alone, there have been very significant changes.

Just take MIT, for example. I've been here for fifty years. When I came—in fact, into the early 1960's—if you walked down the halls at MIT you would have seen white males, formal dress, formal relationships, and so on and so forth. If you walk down the halls today, it's totally different. It's half women, one-third minorities, informal dress, casual relations among people, and a lot of activism of all kinds that never existed. Those are big changes and they were not gifts. Every one of them had to be fought for. And what happened here happened throughout society, in fact in a large part of the world. Those are significant changes and they are advances toward freedom and justice.

Take freedom of speech, which is what one might call a core value. The United States happens to be in the lead in the world in the protection of freedom of speech. But it was not true through history. It was not given in the bill of rights. Maybe some nice words were there, but they weren't implemented. It wasn't until the 20th century that freedom of speech became an issue serious enough to reach the Supreme Court. And, in fact, the early statements of the court on it, when you look back, were not that wonderful. They were usually dissents. Actually, the strong protection for freedom of speech was reached in 1964 in a case involving the civil rights movement. In that case, the Supreme Court did declare unconstitutional the Sedition Acts that went back to 1798, and set a high standard for the protection of freedom of speech which was then improved a few years later. But that indicates how rights are won. It's the same struggle. We can do the same thing now, and it's easier for us now than it has been in the past because we have those victories behind us. There are no particular magic keys about it. There's no secret about how to proceed. It is just a question of will and choice.

Let's keep to MIT. Right now, there is this huge April 2006 issue, big headlines, of Iran's programs of uranium enrichment. As far as is known, they're within legal limits under the Non-Proliferation Treaty. But there is suspicion, which is probably justified, that they are not. However, those very same programs that the U.S. now demands be terminated, were supported by the United States in the 1970's. In fact, right here at MIT, with government support and probably government initiative, the administration agreed to train Iranian nuclear engineers in return for some subsidy from the Shah. At that time, Secretary of State Henry Kissinger stated that Iran should preserve its hydrocarbon resources for other uses and develop nuclear energy because of its need for power. Henry Kissinger, today, says something different. He says that Iran has plenty of oil, so if it's developing nuclear power, it must be for nuclear weapons. He actually was asked why his position is diametrically opposed to what it was in 1977 and his answer was very frank. He said Iran was an ally then, so they needed nuclear energy. Now they're not an ally, so they don't need nuclear energy. Anyway, there was a big furor on campus and it led to a lot of student protests. The students finally had a referendum and they overwhelmingly voted against it. That led to a major faculty meeting in which the faculty overwhelmingly voted for it. The policy was never implemented, but it was approved. So these are things right here, these are constant struggles, that go on.

Actually, the student activism in the 60's had a tremendous influence on MIT. It changed the Institute enormously. MIT was a pretty quiescent campus right through the 60's, one of the more quiet ones. By the late 60's, that began to change, and change very significantly. The most dramatic change was the establishment of a sanctuary for a Marine deserter, organized by a few activists on campus. One of them went on to be elected head of the student body and has done a great many things since. There was a small sanctuary, a couple of dozen students, and within a few days the Institute was virtually closed down. The student center became a place for 24-hour seminars, or rock concerts—anything you could think of—and the Institute was barely functioning. That went on for two weeks. It led to a formal day of cancellation of classes on March 4th, 1969. That day was devoted to considering questions that really hadn't been discussed much, namely, the social responsibility of people working with technology and science. Well, it changed the tone of the Institute significantly in ways that last to the present.

Would you like to see similar alertness in the student body today?

Well, there is quite a lot actually. But there have been many punitive measures taken since then to try to prevent student activism. Not just at MIT, but nationally. One of them is an effort to ensure that students are burdened with debt, so costs have gone up and loans are hard to get. If students are burdened with debt, then when they graduate they are financially trapped, and that directs them into passive and obedient pursuits. I don't have internal documents on it, but I'm sure it was planned. And there are other devices to try to restore obedience. A lot of that was pretty explicit.

The activism of the 1960's caused tremendous concern among the educated classes in general, including liberals. In fact, there is a very important discussion about this that should be widely read. There are many copies of the book in the MIT library because I ordered a lot of them figuring it would probably go out of print pretty soon, which it did. This is the study by the Trilateral Commission called, *The Crisis of Democracy*. Let me indicate the character of those involved. These are not reactionaries. These are liberal internationalists. It was essentially the people who staffed the Carter administration. In fact, it was entirely drawn from that group. Trilateral meant the major three industrial areas of the United States, Europe, and Japan. The commentators put together a report, in which they declared that there was a crisis of democracy in all three places. The crisis was that there was too much democracy. During the 1960's, groups that were usually marginalized and passive began to enter the political arena, the public arena, to press their demands. They were called special interest groups. These groups included women, the young, the elderly, workers, and farmers. They were, in fact, the population. Those were the special interests. There is one group that isn't mentioned in this study, namely, concentrated private power, the corporate sector. They're not mentioned. That's because it is tacitly assumed that they are the national interest, so they're supposed to direct policy. But the special interests were having too much of an influence and that puts too much pressure on the state. The state just could not deal with all these interests. Therefore they called for more moderation in democracy. They proposed various means, but one of them was specifically relevant to schools. They said that institutions were responsible for the indoctrination of the young—that's their phrase, not mine. That includes the schools, the universities, the churches, and so on. They said these institutions were not meeting the responsibility of the indoctrination of the young and if they don't meet that responsibility more effectively, state power will have to move in to do something about that. Well, it didn't lead to policy but it reflected the mood among the liberal sectors. The right-wing was much more extreme, of course. As a matter of fact, many changes took place at that time to try to reverse the crisis of democracy, to keep the public from participating too much in the formation of public policy. These are serious issues and we're in the middle of it right now.

What recent changes have affected your work?

In the public arena, there have been some significant changes. Public policy is formulated within a pretty narrow spectrum, and the intellectual community, in its commentary and discussion and perception of it, also functions within a very narrow spectrum. That's always been true, not just here, but almost everywhere. So just to give an illustration, let's take the Vietnam War. It was a huge issue that blew up the whole country. There is a lot of scholarship on it, a ton of commentary, and it all stays pretty well within a narrow bound. We have what are called doves and hawks. The hawks say it was a noble cause and if we'd fought harder we could have won. The doves say we entered with benign intentions, but it was a mistake—we didn't understand the situation, it was too costly, and we shouldn't have done it. But apart from that spectrum is 70% of the American population, which by 1969 held that the war was fundamentally wrong and immoral. And that has remained pretty true.

So you have a spectrum, but there is another point of view. The other point of view says that aggression is wrong. In fact, people were hanged for it at Nuremberg. There is no doubt that the Kennedy administration invaded and attacked South Vietnam in 1962 and the war expanded into the rest of Indochina. They did it for reasons that are pretty well understood. They were worried that an independent Vietnam would become what is sometimes called a contagious example. In other words, it might infect others. When you have a virus that might infect others, the policies are to destroy the virus and inoculate the others. That was done. Vietnam was destroyed and the surrounding countries were inoculated by the imposition of vicious and murderous tyrannies which were greeted with euphoria. Well, that is another point of view, but that point of view just can't enter the discussion. The discussion has to keep to the dove/hawk spectrum.

The same is true on Iraq. There are critics of the war on Iraq who say it was a mistake, we didn't understand it, and so on. To try to find a critic that brings up the Nuremberg judgment, you'd have to go pretty far out. That is considered extremely radical. So, in other words, taking the deeply conservative position that we should adhere to international law and our own values is considered extremely radical and practically off the spectrum. Well, it tells you something about intellectual life.

Now, within this narrow spectrum there are differences. The Bush administration happens to be at a radical nationalist extreme of the narrow spectrum. It's true domestically and internationally. Domestically, they are dedicated to trying to dismantle the achievements of popular struggle over the last century: social welfare measures, freedom and democracy, and so on. Internationally, they want to terrify the world into submission. That is why the U.S. is carrying out policies of aggressive militarism that really are frightening the world and creating plenty of fear and hatred of the United States. They're also consciously enhancing the threat of terror. Not because they want it, but because they don't care very much. They are enhancing the threat of nuclear war and enhancing the threat of environmental disaster. The main policy is pretty simple. Stuff as many dollars as you can in the pockets of your rich friends and forget about what happens tomorrow. Well, those are extreme positions and, yes, they've changed immediate concerns.

The technologies that have most influenced activism are computers and the Internet. These happen to be, largely, MIT products. There is a common myth that the United States is a free market, free enterprise society. That is very far from true. The economy depends very extensively on the dynamic state sector of the economy, of which MIT is a core part. Research and development, in the difficult stages, are typically carried out at public expense. For a long time it was under the pretext of defense. So up until the 1970's, I suppose, MIT was funded mostly by the Pentagon—something like 90%. Well, it wasn't producing arms. It was producing the economy of the future. It was developing computers, the Internet, information technology, telecommunications, and so on. That continued for a long period of time. Computers were being developed from the early 50's under government contracts, at MIT mainly, and at Harvard and other places. It wasn't until about 1980 that companies could start selling them for money.

The Internet was in the public sector for thirty years before it was handed over to the private sector. Right now, there are efforts underway to try to restrict the use of the Internet, to try to prevent people from using it for activist and other purposes, to direct them in particular paths. That is a big problem coming up. But the point is that all of this technology, which has been very significant, came out of the state sector, a lot of it right here at MIT, and it certainly has changed activism enormously. Take publication. Publishing used to be a very expensive enterprise. Now poor Third World countries or small activist groups can do desktop publishing for almost nothing. I've seen that at work. One of my daughters has been working in a Third World country for years. The Internet is the major mode of interaction and communication.

The global justice movement is unique in history. It's the first time in history there has ever been a massive international movement working for globalization. In conventional terminology, they are called "anti-globalization," because the term "globalization" is appropriated by the doctrinal system to refer to a specific form of international integration designed for the benefit of investors. The global justice movement is committed to international integration in the interests of people, and therefore is called "anti-globalization." If one compares participation in the World Social Forum and the World Economic Forum, which meets at the same time, it is pretty clear which organization is more representative of the world population, but—or maybe, therefore—it is ignored or derided within the doctrinal system.

In the World Social Forum, there are a huge number of people all organized on the Internet. The Internet enables people to circumvent the control over media content and opinion imposed by the concentrated corporate sector of the media. It is the tool of organization, education, and activism. So that is one use of technology. Of course, it also has very negative uses. But technology is, by and large, very neutral. It's kind of like a hammer. You can use it to build a house or you can use it to bash someone's head in. The hammer doesn't care. Most technology is available for constructive or destructive uses. After that, it's a matter of human choice.

Where do you see your work in a global context? Where do you see it going?

All I can see is that when I go home tonight, I'll have five hours of email to answer, and at least an hour of it will be turning down invitations that I wish I could take but can't. And it goes years ahead. 9/11 was a point of inflection, and it was substantial. 9/11 did open a lot of people's minds. But what the effect is, that's for others to say.

Interviewed 4/25/06

SUZANNE BERGER

Raphael Dorman and Helen Starbuck Professor of Political Science
Director of the MIT International Science and Technology Initiatives

What are you working on here at MIT?

For the last five years, I've been working on understanding what the changes in the international economy are going to mean for the general well-being of our own society. I've been working on this in two ways.

One is a research project with colleagues here at MIT, involving both engineers and social scientists. The latest product of that research is a book called *How We Compete.* We did over 700 interviews in which we talked to managers in companies around the world and tried to understand how they decide what they're going to offshore, what they're going to outsource, and what they're going to leave in their own home societies. And what we've discovered, which is really quite fascinating, is that even for companies making the same products, there are very diverse solutions. I think what makes us all feel very anxious about globalization is the possibility that it may limit our choices as individuals and as citizens. Maybe it forces all countries and all companies onto the same very narrow path and into a race to the bottom on wages and standards. But our research shows that there really is space for choice, and the different choices companies make can have very different and significant implications for quality of work, levels of employment, and innovative capabilities.

The second project has to do with education at MIT. If you understand the tremendous transformation of the international economy, you realize that twenty years ago when students graduated from MIT and went to work for a company, most or all of their activities would take place between the four walls of that one company. Furthermore, that company was quite likely to be within the United States, so people didn't think they needed to know very much about the rest of the world. But over the last twenty years, there has been a fragmentation of production systems, so that today, even when someone goes to work for an American company, how well they do over their lifetime will have to do with how well they coordinate resources and capabilities that are distributed around the world. That means that people have to understand in a very deep way how people in the rest of world create products and knowledge. Without that international understanding, it will be impossible to do a job well. So we've created at MIT a program called the MIT International Science and Technology Initiatives. Currently, we're focusing on eight

countries. We've started with Japan, China, India, Mexico, France, Italy, Germany, and Spain. The idea is to give our students a chance, in their own disciplines and in the areas of their own interest, to gain hands-on experience as interns or in research teams outside of the U.S.

In many ways, these two projects are complementary and feed off of each other. And that's what's compelling about being at a place like MIT. Research and teaching do converge in a very interesting way.

What changes in your field have affected your research today?

Well, I'm in the Department of Political Science. In the structure of MIT, departments endure eternally. Departments are the places where faculty members are appointed, candidates are admitted, and students earn degrees. However, research centers, which cut across the Institute, come and go. Although I've always been in political science, my research interests and activities have been diverse. I've been involved with the Center for International Studies and the Industrial Performance Center. There have also been collaborations with colleagues who often are not in political science. I think I belong to all of these intellectual communities.

Certainly, on this globalization project there have been enormous changes over the last twenty years. We now have a different view than we had two decades ago of what is the strongest way to organize production, research, and innovation. Twenty years ago, a group of MIT faculty from across the Institute studied competitiveness and economic performance, and wrote a book together called *Made In America*. The driver was our desire to understand why American companies were not doing very well. This was at the end of the 1980's. We looked at Japan and Germany, and at that time it seemed that companies that did the best were those that could bring research, development, design, and production into close proximity, and thereby get close to their most important customers and suppliers. Today, as I said before, everything has to do with the ability to understand and to pull together resources that are distributed across the world. It's a completely different sort of puzzle. We have to figure out how to educate people in a world where what is going to be required of them is the ability to identify knowledge and value wherever they are being created and to coordinate globally distributed activities.

Now, if we look at what is driving globalization, we could probably all agree on the big drivers. There has been a significant liberalization of trade and financial markets. We've seen the rise of major new competitors in China and India, and new technologies in communication and transportation. The result has been a tremendous increase in the flow of capital, goods, and services across borders. As a result, with the rise of these new competitors, people in our own society worry about what China, India, and the emergence of yet other countries means for our jobs and our children. But how could we really desire the alternative, which is a world where billions of people remain stuck on the bottom of the ladder?

The main contribution that we can make at a place like MIT is, at least, to try to understand systematically what is happening and changing. Much of what people think they know is based on anecdotes and very little evidence. One of the things we've discovered is that very few jobs are actually transferred outside of the United States. The U.S. Bureau of Labor Statistics survey in 2003 found only thirteen thousand jobs that were lost in the United States because the job was transferred. Now, there has been a lot of argument about those figures, and some researchers claim that the number could be as high as three or four hundred thousand, but even that is a small drop in an American job market of about 140 million jobs.

So what is important, and what our research would like people to focus on, is what kinds of jobs are going to be created in the United States. It might be not so much that we're losing existing jobs to other places, but that the new jobs that will be created outside of the U.S. are ones that would never see the light of day in our society. The issue is what we can do to create new economic activities and jobs at home. When you look around MIT and Harvard, at the biotech and pharmaceutical companies, and you realize that they're setting up in these old factory buildings with high rents, in a state with high taxes, and with workers who earn high wages, you wonder why they would want to be here. The answer is, because they have to be next to the labs at MIT and Harvard that are pouring out innovation. I think the real question is, what creates an environment so favorable that jobs locate there because people know that it is absolutely the best place to be? In other words, not because wages are low, or social benefits are low, but because the advantages and strengths of being in that locality are so high.

Where do you see your work in a global context? Where do you see it going?

I think fears about globalization are widely shared around the world. For example, as my colleague Professor Edward Steinfeld, an expert on China, has pointed out, just as we are afraid of the impact of the expansion of China on American job industries, the Chinese are equally afraid of the consequences of opening their own markets. And, in fact, the number of jobs in industry has gone down in China, not up. So the question of what kind of impact opening borders to the international flow of goods, services, and capital is likely to have is a question that is being asked around the world. Last week, the French translation of *How We Compete* came out. I was in France discussing it, and it was just striking to me how many of these same questions people are asking there. People were quite astonished to realize that even in the United States, where we've gained such enormous benefits from globalization, we too have deep anxieties about this. So there really are common themes and common questions that show this is not simply an American issue.

Globalization produces winners and losers everywhere. The problem is, if you lose your job, if you are someone who is forty years old and you have a manufacturing job in the United States and you've been working for GM or Ford, the likelihood is that you will never again find a job that pays the same salary, with the same medical benefits, and the same pension. So for some people, the changes in the economy are going to be flat out losses. And that, unfortunately, is an issue that our society has to yet to deal with adequately. Even if there are benefits for society as a whole, and the benefits are widely distributed in the form of cheaper goods and services, there still will be losers.

What are the implications of your work?

I see implications for MIT and also for public policy. I think the world has changed in such a way that to educate our students well, we need to teach them how to access knowledge and how to contribute to the creation of knowledge around the world. So we have to teach students that they might be working in a lab at MIT that is a more dynamic place than a lab they can find today in China, but that very same lab in China might soon be creating the kind of knowledge that they will need to be able to share. And you can't access that knowledge if you waltz in with your Berlitz book, speak English and hope to cruise through in a day. You need to understand that people pose problems in different ways, people work in teams in different ways, and people arrive at solutions in different ways. So I believe, from my research in globalization, that we should internationalize the education of our students. Hands-on experience in a foreign society has become an essential part of an education.

I think one of our greatest strengths in the United States is openness and willingness to see economic resources recombined and put together in a different way. People are generally willing to let companies go bust if they aren't doing well, and to see the resources reused. But if that means losing a job, and losing your chance of taking care of your family's health, and losing all chance of a decent old age, people are not going to put up with this openness. So I believe that in order to strengthen our own commitments to openness, both within this society and to the outside world, we're going to have to pay a lot more attention to providing the people who live here with the basic guarantees of a decent life.

Interviewed 3/1/06

MUNTADAS

Visiting Professor at the MIT Visual Arts Program

What are you working on here at MIT?

I usually work on a number of different projects at the same time. Some projects are at the very beginning stages of production, others are in the middle, and still others are ready to be shown. I've been involved with MIT, in different relationships and in different periods, since 1977. In a sense, I consider it my alma mater. I have always found it to be a good source and place for dialogue. The environment is unique and we who teach here have privileged access to information. Therefore, over the years I have developed many projects here, most of which have been interdisciplinary in their inception and growth.

In 1979, I developed a project called *Subjectivity.* It consisted of a book and videotape about TV and was exhibited at the Hayden Gallery as an installation. That was about the interpretation of images. The images I used were taken from mass media—from LIFE magazine, actually. I sent letters with photographs to 250 people in different parts of the world and asked each of them to write a subtitle, or caption, for the picture. The result was a book called *Subjectivity: 50 Photographs from the Best of Life.* It was published here at MIT and is an examination of how an image can be subjectively interpreted in so many different ways by different people in different parts of the world. At the end of the book I included the original captions, photography credits, and names of the contributors.

More recently, I have produced a number of separate projects all connected to the idea of translation. In this case, MIT's main function was to serve as a base for research. One project, *On Translation: Fear/Miedo,* was produced at the border between Tijuana and San Diego. It is part of the larger *On Translation* series, which grew out of my interest to show how we live in a totally translated world. I'm not talking about translation from one language to another, but translation in terms of cultures, economics, societies, politics, and of course, media. Perhaps this project gives a better sense of the kind of work I'm doing now.

On Translation: Fear/Miedo focused on the situation at the border between Tijuana and San Diego and investigated how fear was interpreted on each side. The fear of the people in Mexico near the border is completely different from the fear experienced on the American side. The fear on the south side is the fear of physical repression, violence,

and the uncertainties inherent in the search for a better quality of life. The fear on the north side is fear of the unknown—in other words, fear of cultural differences and foreign language. The project is thirty minutes long and was produced for television. We're showing it not only in Tijuana and San Diego, but also in the capitals, Mexico City and Washington D.C. Sometimes I feel that when we talk about the border, we forget that the lines extend all the way to the capitals. That is to say, the decisions that affect the people and towns on both sides of the border are coming from Washington D.C. and Mexico City.

The sensation and emotion of fear is something that is relevant to all parts of the world. The relationship of architecture and fear is actually the main theme of the course on public art I'm currently teaching called, "The Disappearance of Public Space: The Construction of Fear." I think recently there has been a lot of interest in and projects about the notion of the city as a territory, how cities are constructed in terms of various devices of control—for instance, how gated communities encroach on city centers, increasing the sense of paranoia, which then has a spin-off effect throughout other social and political arenas. I feel strongly that the political discourse in many parts of the world, and particularly in the United States, is guided by the politics of fear. This is related to how the fight against terrorism is pursued and how opinion is shaped in the media.

What recent changes in or around your field affect your work today?

The works are always autobiographical. One's interests are related to one's own concerns. The social or political concerns that come up on a personal level are then transferred to my work. All the works have this edge, but each from a different perspective, because the projects I like to work on are very much produced in response to specific places. Every project is defined by its context, the working process, and the medium. In my case, the evolution was to go from more generic issues to an examination of trans-national topics through the lens of a specific local situation. It's like zooming in and zooming out again, from the local level to the global level. But again, the context is always important, not only in terms of where the project comes from, but also in terms of where it is going to be presented.

Where do you see your work in a global context? How do you see it evolving in the future?

Well, some projects have to do with global issues. I'm talking about mass media and the city as general problems. But, as I said earlier, I'm moving from the general idea of a city to the specific idea of a particular city. I begin by looking at site-specific and context-specific variables, but ultimately arrive at a work that has more to do with problems and issues on a larger scale.

I'm a curious person. I dedicate time to a project because I want to learn from the project. I always work from a sense of curiosity and a desire to learn. After a certain period of time, I shift to another thing, not because I know everything, but perhaps that project transports me to something else. It's a continuum. The *On Translation* series was started in 1995. Since then I have produced more than 38 works for it. I feel though that it still has the capacity to grow and I am motivated to do more new works. I like the idea of a series because the works complement each other and encourage the viewer to consider the common threads.

Do you see downsides to your work?

The nature of working with projects is that some get done and some don't. There are many reasons why this happens. Some projects are commissioned and therefore can be finished easily. With other works, in a sense, you commission yourself. Sometimes a project will remain unfinished because you are waiting for the appropriate time, or waiting to find a situation or environment where it belongs. But I'm pretty stubborn and persistent when it comes to pursuing a work. Regardless of the hurdles, sooner or later the projects get done.

Do you feel that they are received properly and understood?

This is another story. Especially with projects in a public space, you have to deal with the idea that seeing is not necessarily perceiving. The desire of artists to work in the public space has to do with the notion that more people can access the work. But do they really perceive it? It's a risk that the artist takes. How do people encounter the work in the public sphere? How do they navigate around it? This idea that greater accessibility can often correlate to greater ambivalence is an interesting and profound paradox.

Interviewed 3/6/07

LEON ROBERT GLICKSMAN

Professor of Building Technology and Mechanical Engineering
Head of the Building Technology Program in the Department of Architecture

What are you working on here at MIT?

Primarily, we are working on issues related to environmental sustainability within the urban construction environment. A key feature of that is energy efficiency, particularly as it relates to buildings, indoor air quality, and quality of life for people within buildings. We teach people about sustainable building concepts, try to persuade them to employ these concepts, and hopefully reach the point where those in and around construction recognize the pursuit of these goals as vital and necessary.

What is the current state of building technology in the United States and in the world?

It varies from country to country. In Western Europe, particularly in Germany, people are much more aware of environmental issues. They really have done a better job of including sustainable concepts in some of the new buildings that are being erected. In the U.S., that awareness is just beginning.

Let me give you an example. Are you familiar with the Genzyme building on the other side of campus?

No.

On the outside it looks like a fairly ordinary building, but on the inside it is absolutely wonderful. It employs a number of new sustainable concepts such as means of bringing in daylight and using natural ventilation to provide better indoor air quality. There are a few good examples of this type of thinking here in the U.S., but so far it has been the exception rather than the rule. Unfortunately, in most of the U.S. developments the primary concern is lowest first cost. People don't yet realize the significant advantages inherent in sustainability.

We recently had a major program in China, which we worked on for about five years, trying to promote sustainable residential buildings. They are building there at an incredible rate, something like 10 to 12 million new residential units per year. Unfortunately, most of the developers are not yet concerned with these issues. They talk about green projects,

as most architects in the U.S. do, but in many cases they don't understand what that really encompasses.

Could you mention a particular project that you are working on now?

Right now there are two projects that we have under way. In one, we're doing work on natural ventilation in commercial buildings. Most modern office buildings are sealed up boxes. The claim is that they can be more easily air-conditioned for, supposedly, better comfort. We're trying to demonstrate that if you design properly, you can have buildings with operable windows and large open spaces, and people will still be quite comfortable.

In the second project, we are developing computer software that will predict the energy advantages of different designs. Heretofore, the software for this task has been developed by engineers for other engineers and been too difficult for architects to understand and employ. So we are trying to develop user-friendly yet sophisticated software that architects can to use to evaluate the implications of their construction choices.

Have there been any changes in your field in the recent past, or in general, that affect your research today?

Because of the sudden spike in energy prices, people are becoming more aware of energy issues. In the past, there has been a lot of individual effort to penetrate the public consciousness, but we are now realizing a need for a more integrated approach. That is exactly what we have tried to do here. We've got engineers, architects, and urban planners all working together on a number of different projects.

Technologically, are any changes that have happened outside of your field influencing the choice of materials?

Yes. Professor John Fernandez, in our group, is doing work on a material selector. Again, this is software which will allow architectural designers to choose from a larger pallet of materials than have been traditionally employed in the past. In this case, the question is whether they can use and apply the advanced materials that have been developed for other areas—for example, aircraft and automobile industries. Professor Marilyne Andersen, also in our group, has been doing work to develop materials and designs in order to bring daylight deeper into buildings and replace the need for artificial lights.

What role do you see your work playing in a global context and how do you see it evolving?

As I mentioned, there is the work we've done in China, and the natural ventilation work has been in coordination with people in the UK. Where would we like it to go? Our hope is that we will have an international impact on design decisions for future buildings.

Regarding policy recommendations, what kinds of experiences have you had both here and overseas?

Encouraging people to do this type of thing is even more important than the technology. To this end, we are working to develop demonstration projects which show people that these ideas are valid and can be implemented economically. We are also pushing for more stringent codes and standards so that people are forced to alter their methods accordingly.

What are the implications of the implementation of your work?

If we are successful, people will be happier in their living and working environments. We will have better air quality, better lighting, and more comfortable surroundings. As a result, people will be more productive and more interested in working and learning. The downside is that it is just not going to happen very fast. It's going to take a lot of effort.

Interviewed 5/9/06

ROSALIND WILLIAMS

Bern Dibner Professor of the History of Science and Technology
Director of the Program in Science, Technology, and Society (until July 1, 2006)

What are you working on here at MIT?

I'm working on what I always work on. I have one big question I always come back to. What is it like to live in a world that's primarily self-created? So much in our surroundings reflects human desires, energies, aspirations, and powers. This is a very different world from the one human beings have inhabited for most of the millennia of our existence. What does this mean for human life?

When I first came to MIT, in the early 1980's, I had just finished a book on consumer society. I was interested in the idea of consumer society as a world of merchandise, where people are in their created spaces and are immersed in commercial products. I followed that with a work of imaginative literature involving underground fantasies. I had noticed that there is a theme of underground living running through a great deal of 19th century Western literature. The paradox of that existence is that though you are in the heart of nature, quite literally, survival in the underworld is impossible without the abilities to generate light, food, and water. Therefore, you depend entirely on technological systems. If they break down, you're doomed. Often in these stories, the reason for retreating underground is some environmental or military catastrophe which has ruined the earth. It fascinated me to consider what it would be like to live in a completely technologically based environment. Again, what is it like to live in a world that's primarily built, rather than given?

At that point in my career, I made what some might consider a detour. I went into administration here at MIT and worked as Dean of Students and Undergraduate Education for five years in the late 1990's. It turned out to be not such a detour after all. At the outset, I often wondered what I was doing in this job. One of the answers I arrived at was that I felt I could get a good book out of it, which is the way a writer always thinks. That book, *Retooling: A Historian Confronts Technological Change,* was about the built world, and it focused on MIT as the site of that world.

There are so many people at MIT who devote themselves to creating objects, processes, and actions that become part of all our lives. So, in writing that book about MIT, and because MIT is fundamentally about engineering, my major inquiry was what is happening

to engineering as a profession, as a discipline, and as a calling. Why is engineering different in a primarily built world? Nature is not dead or gone, it's just so mixed in with human creations that you can't tell the two apart. Global warming is a perfect example. Nobody disputes that it's happening. The only dispute is what proportion of what is happening is generated by human beings.

What has substantially changed?

The term we use in the trade to describe this situation is *reflexive*. This is a reflexive world where what you do goes out, but also comes back to you. For example, I have a whole chapter in *Retooling* on new software programs that were brought into MIT in the 1990's to handle finances and accounting. There was quite a bit of resistance to this here, some of which was understandable. That experiment fascinated me because it was an example of reflexivity. MIT takes such pride in being first and foremost in electrical engineering and computer science, being pioneers in inventing all these processes and programs. But there was a real resistance to having old MIT habits change to conform to the requirements of the new software. Innovation never comes back as just a technology, it comes back as a society. The social aspects of reengineering, as the process was called, in many ways challenged the MIT ethos. Reengineering made a wonderful case study. What goes out can look very different when it comes back. You have to find a way to live with it.

I have come back to literature as a way of understanding the change from a given world to a built world in the 19th century. The 19th century is essentially the first era of globalization. This is the era where, by almost every measurement and criterion, there's a takeoff point in terms of energy consumption, resource use, and other impacts of the human footprint on the planet. These changes have been studied and recorded by environmental historians. The time around the turn of the 20th century is a critical moment in human history. I'm interested though not in the changes as they've been described in physical terms, but how people have responded to them socially, culturally, and psychologically. For these combined and complicated responses, literature is one of the best records we have.

What recent changes in and around your field affect your research today?

I'm a historian. For many years, dating back to when I was in college, I have specialized in history and literature, specifically literature as it illuminates history. I am interested in the cultural history of technology and how people have responded to the technological world and concepts of technology. But I'm also in the STS program, a program that studies technology and society. STS itself is a blend of the history of technology, history of science, social studies of science and technology, anthropology, sociology, and philosophy, among others.

Interest is stirred by current events. I think there is no question about that. If you look at environmental history—which isn't quite what I do, though my work is certainly on the border—while people were certainly working on this back in the 20's and 30's, there really isn't a takeoff point until the late 70's and early 80's. The events that can be described as the flowering of the environmental movement, such as the publication of Rachel Carson's *Silent Spring* and the establishment of the Environmental Protection Agency, are all clustered in the late 60's and early 70's. Scholars pay attention to what is going on in the world. The same is true with the development of the history of technology.

In the 1980's, there was a real sense within STS of being marginalized, both at MIT and in the larger world. The idea of looking at the impact of science and technology on society, and the impact of society on technology, was not of great interest to many people outside this unit. But in the last seven or eight years the situation has changed dramatically. It now seems normal that if you are going to work on energy issues, for example, you must not only consider technology in a narrow sense, but also consumption, law, and politics. To my taste, it's still not enough and I believe MIT needs to go further in this direction. The big problems faced by humanity are not just technological issues, but involve large social systems. Because this is a fairly recent idea, there is a bit of a lag between the awareness of the complexity of these issues and the social and political structures to address them—that is, we don't have the structures to support the awareness. A big question now is how long we can keep using new technologies to fix complicated sets of problems caused by earlier technologies.

What do you think?

This is no one answer. This is a question about the limits of human ability to control this environment, which is now predominantly human built and therefore very complicated and unpredictable. I think a sober awareness of the limits of our ability to control this world we've built is a significant realization and an important first step. If people are educated to simply consider this idea, we will have come a long way. As a historian, my observation is that history works differently now because of this environment we've created for ourselves. The stage on which the historical drama takes place is no longer a stable one. Our actions have changed it. We have atomic processes which create waste that has a half-life of 20,000 years. This is out of proportion with all human historical time scales. What kind of society will we have in 20,000 years? What are the consequences of global warming or genetic modifications? These issues are unprecedented, as is our capacity to change the world we live in. There is a range of consequences to our behavior and it is not possible for anyone to say whether they're all good or all bad. It is necessary for people to recognize what powers and forces are at work, and that the capacity to control them is something that we cannot necessarily achieve.

Where do you see your work in a global context? Where do you see it going?

To be honest, I've never thought of my work as being on the theme of globalization. That said, in some ways the book I'm writing now is about global history, with the late 19th century as a pivot point. The thing that is different about the late 19th century is that, for the first time, people saw the end of the global frontier—not just the American frontier in the West. One could look at the map of the world and still see some empty spaces, especially at the poles, but also know that people will eventually get everywhere, and they did. People were now beginning to see the globe as complete, finished, and full. It was not an exhilarating moment at all. It was a very sobering moment because of the realization that there was no other place to go. You have to deal with the idea that this is the world, these are the people on it, and there's no more beyond—in the material or, even possibly, the spiritual sense. This realization happened concurrently with the turn of the century.

I'm very interested in how people think about the globe. Of course, everybody lives locally, so even if you talk about globalization as a concept, you're still experiencing it in a specific place. Furthermore, in the late 19th century, it is impossible to separate globalization from imperialism. They're not identical, but they overlap so much that it is impossible to sort them out neatly.

I'm also very interested in artists, especially imaginative writers. For instance, Joseph Conrad begins *Heart of Darkness* in the estuary of the Thames, sitting there watching the sunset, knowing they're going to be setting sail for Africa, and imagining the time when Romans were the colonizers of what is now England. Estuaries in particular are interesting to me because that's where the ebb and flow literally happens. In my current book, I'm looking at a cluster of late 19th century writers who were all writing about, among other things, the relationship between land and water. This relationship is important to the way they saw and experienced globalization.

There's quite a lot of literature and history about this period as the first era of globalization. Susan Berger, in the Political Science Department, has written a book on this topic, but it's in French so most people here haven't read it. Her case, and she's not alone in making the argument, is that in the later 19th century—between steam ships at sea, the railroad on land, and then the undersea telegraph—the world was wired in a way unlike ever before. It was not as fast as today, not instantaneous, but it was such a dramatic step beyond anything that had come previously. It was revolutionary. It's still revolutionary. Communications are so much faster now, but the real moments of invention were then. The real invention is having the message going by telegraph rather than by messenger. You can argue that the rest is all an expansion on that theme.

Do you think we are now fostering the deleterious effects of technology?

The anxieties about where things are headed are very much part of the common vocabulary. You don't need a historian to invent them. Where is the world population going to peak? What is the demand on resources going to be? What are the normal accidents—to use a phrase from the sociology of technology—that we can expect in terms of viruses or military catastrophes or unpredictable effects?

I said earlier that history works differently now. Maybe I should restate that. You have old-fashioned history going on as usual—that's the story of power, resources, aggression, and conflict. But it is layered on this new history in which human beings have begun processes with no idea of where they're going to stop. It's a very unstable situation.

The immense energies we are able to marshal now are going into material development. That will continue, and you can expect that to make a lot of demands on all resources. What social developments might dramatically change our sense of values and priorities? That's harder to predict. Such changes in values and priorities happen continuously throughout history, but this is something that can never be predicted. You can say what might happen, but you can never say for sure.

What are the implications of your work? Are there downsides?

The notion that progress has a price is very old. In other words, there are few people who are unabashed believers in progress and don't acknowledge any downsides. The downside I'm interested in is what progress does to our planet, our world we love. I don't just mean in terms of pollution, I mean as a setting for a human existence that considers values, feelings, and experiences as much a part of human necessity as energy, food, or water. We've evolved for millions of years on this planet. We're exquisitely tuned to it. We all have a long adjustment period after our birth, getting in touch with our surroundings, with the rhythms of the seasons, and with the nonhuman nature that surrounds us. This is an evolutionary fact, this set of experiences. We cannot then just opt for a new self-created habitat. It's not that easy.

I'm interested in the price material progress exacts on the human experience. If you look at the lifespan of an ordinary human being, which keeps getting longer and longer, and you look at the pace of change in the physical world, they're out of sync entirely. We've lost a certain stability that people have counted on for many, many years. That point of reference is gone. That is an enormous loss. In fact, the more you experience progress in a material sense, the more you experience loss. This sense of loss should not be dismissed as sentimentalism or anti-progress, and my work is about trying to find a vocabulary to validate those experiences. That's very hard to do at a place like MIT. But if we don't accept certain aspects of reality, then we're going to end up with an environment that is not only not particularly natural, but also not particularly human.

Interviewed 5/15/07

KRZYSZTOF WODICZKO

Professor of Visual Arts
Director of the Center for Advanced Visual Studies
Head of the Interrogative Design Group

What are you working on here at MIT?

Perhaps I'll begin with some past work and then talk about present plans. *Dis-Armor* is a project that was developed for Japanese high school students. It was conceived and created here under the umbrella of the Interrogative Design Group, which I established here at the Center for Advanced Visual Studies and in which I'm a leading person. Initially, the city of Hiroshima asked me to come up with a proposal to build a sculpture in the city. This was connected to the Hiroshima Prize I received. I managed to spend some time in Japan while preparing my exhibition and special projection projects, and began learning about various problems young people have to live with there, specifically the tensions that exist between that demographic and the rest of society. I soon discovered that the root of all these problems was poor communication.

So here at the Interrogative Design Group—with the help of Adam Whiton, Sung Ho Kim, other members, and graduate students—I developed a proposal for a piece of equipment that would help young people communicate their anxieties, doubts, criticisms, and existential quandaries to anybody they could approach in public space. This piece of equipment, also developed with help from local school teachers, school psychologists, psychoanalysts, and other specialists on the problems of young people in Japan, was specifically geared to a particular group of kids known as school refusers—a group of young people that refuse to participate in the school system.

The project is based on the suggestion, popular in Japan, that one can learn about what someone is thinking by looking at that person's back. Presumably, it is more than can be learned by looking at the face. So, by combining different pieces of equipment and various types of available technology, we armed those young people with the possibility of communicating—in pre-recorded mode and in real-time mode—through their backs. We transmitted their eyesight to their backs through a special headpiece equipped with video cameras pointed at the user's eyes, then added monitors, a speaker, and a microphone. A computer allows pre-recorded speech to be triggered, or replayed, in a particular moment of conversation or contact with the interlocutor who is standing behind. An additional rearview mirror—and later, camera and monitor—enabled the young people to see behind themselves. The equipment has other features as well, including the possibility of walking

and speaking in tandem, with one person carrying the other person's voice and eyes, and vice versa.

This project illustrates the kind of direction we're trying to take here, which is to create a transitory, intermediate technological interface between people who have difficulties opening up and sharing experiences with others. It also allows others to come closer and therefore gain a better understanding of those experiences. The common aspect of these projects is that they are operated in public or semi-public space. These works create an opportunity for communication technology to function as an interface between alienated parties in our societies. They allow those who usually have no voice the opportunity to develop the capacity to communicate, and allow others to develop the capacity to listen. The step-by-step process of learning how to use the equipment, and the journey toward eventual operational virtuosity, enhances one's ability to perform, express, find gesture in, and impart emotional charge to one's own testimony. One might say these devices are cultural, psycho-cultural, and political prostheses. They may function as memory prostheses, or aids, as well.

The political, ethical, and psychological aspects of this endeavor are just as important as the technological aspect. It sounds very complex, and there may be an overly optimistic or utopian strain to projects like this, but these are modest attempts to help potentially fearless speakers animate public space with a meaningful and critical intervention, and also bring some life to public space itself. We are encouraging people to insert their voices not only into our silent physical public space, but also into the media space. By virtue of their transmission into a forum where they are apprehended by millions, these projects are able to transcend physical, public environment.

In Japan, this project was presented as quite a long television film. It was also presented in museums and reported by television, radio and press. Those young people used our equipment to learn how to speak and communicate, and the media used the performance to magnify an important social issue, which is the alienation of those people. It provoked quite a heated discussion. This film caused a lot of trouble. There were protests. Some of the protests actually came from members of the psychoanalytical community. In reality though, without equipment like this, the youth would not have been able to speak so effectively and other people would not have had the occasion and opportunity to listen. Interestingly, although some of the issues spoken about related to subjects often considered taboo in Japanese culture—such as, public discussion of family relationships and domestic problems—even the parents of those children were quite positive about it. Despite all of the problems, the film was presented by a main television network. This affirmed both its own right to exist in public space and the right of those young people to be heard. Through this process, the potential cultural and social benefits of projects such as this one became quite evident. We're actually working now, in a very preliminary stage, on similar equipment for veterans of the war in Iraq.

What recent changes in and around your field have affected your work?

A different type of work I've been developing over many years is the animation of symbolic city structures—such as, public monuments, edifices, statues and facades—through projection. We use the technology of large-scale projection of sound and video to temporarily imbue prestigious civic structures with the presence of alienated or marginalized city residents. In so doing, we recognize that there are urban residents who are monumentally silent, frozen in incapacitation, living monuments to their own trauma. We are enlarging the presence of those small residents and also creating a situation in which those who feel large, important, and confident can feel smaller. The goal is to increase contact and therefore diminish distance. We want to equalize a sense of scale that is currently distorted, which is the discrepancy between our perception of ourselves and the symbols we honor, in relation to lesser known citizens and residents. By enlarging the smaller and unknown to the scale of the larger and more familiar symbols, we are creating the possibility of connection.

We are now examining the possibility of appropriating and animating some of the statues in Boston. A few days ago the Institute of Contemporary Art invited me to propose a project for the city. That may be an occasion to develop new research and examine technological options. We may, for instance, use a separate substance that can hold images and also make them appear and disappear. Those techniques of projection—using fog, or some other substance, to hold an image—are very old. They originated in maybe the 17th century with the magic lantern and wandering projectionists who created illusions of biblical scenes and religious holidays, or tried to bring back some dead people in the salons of Paris. There's nothing new about this. It's just that projectors are much more advanced now. We also have a lot of digital equipment and we can create new interfaces that will allow real-time projection, distant projection, wireless technology, and use of the Internet. Additionally, the monuments themselves are hundreds of years old and so, over time, have assumed a variety of meanings. There's also a powerful mass media that can re-transmit these projects.

We now have a greater understanding of the relationship between politics, psychology, and the media. Therefore, we recognize the importance of recovery from trauma and have developed techniques which help people explore these difficult experiences. In other words, when it comes to technology, cultural work, and art, there are myriad new conditions and expectations. Artists have gained more rights and independence. Also, we have a political structure that not merely guarantees, but demands our assertion of communicative rights. That is written in the First Amendment to the Constitution of the United States. The battle over expanding access to those rights for the less privileged is an ongoing conflict in which communication technology and public art can play an active role. In this context, I see our work as an obligation.

Where do you see your work in a global context? Also, how, if at all, does this influence your teaching?

This course called Interrogative Design Workshop is the core of my teaching here. Like most workshops, it is open to and inclusive of students from various pockets of MIT, Harvard, the School of the Museum of Fine Arts, and Massachusetts College of Art. So a few of our graduate art students are working with students from the Media Lab, Cognitive Science, Engineering, Architecture, and other art and design schools. Discussions are quite complex because each of the members of the workshop arrives with disparate skills, interests, and life experiences.

There are also many foreign students and underprivileged students from right here in the U.S., who, in this course, are encouraged to explore their alienation from their friends and families—or explore any difficult periods of their lives—and connect all of that with a range of readings that touch upon elements of psychology, ethics, media theory, cultural theory, philosophy, poetry, and literature. All of those various texts, and other materials by which members of the workshop are surrounded, make them feel not alone. They discover that some of their own life experiences may already be the subject of various discourses. So, we are connecting reading, discussions, and designed projects with their life experiences.

They end up with not always completely finished projects, but at least a vehicle that gives them an opportunity to pursue work in art and design research. Sometimes it evolves into a PhD thesis or becomes their educational focus when they teach. Sometimes they even actually honor it through continued art making. Even if they previously had not been art students, or had never studied art before, this may trigger an interest to take other courses in the art program here. There are always a variety of unexpected outcomes regarding the experiences of students in that workshop. It is not a traditional teaching environment. Here, people are free to connect their own interests and experiences with interpretations of readings and ideas for projects, without any direct instruction or specific exercises given to them. Therefore, the method of those discussions, seminars, and meetings resembles the act of making art in the public space itself. This is an artistic workshop in which projects are developed from scratch and taken as far as they can go. They are not pre-conceived, pedagogical exercises. Because many of the students are used to more structured, rigid education in engineering or architectural programs, it often takes awhile for them to adjust to this method. But in the end, I think it creates a good condition for their own independent creative process, regardless of the field they choose.

What are the downsides of your own research and how you deal with them?

Of course, I have a problem with the fact that in our society and education system, art is not considered a necessary and indispensable part of our experience in the world. But when you consider our philosophical tradition—that is, ideas about how we should perfect ourselves, make sense of our lives, and what type of life we should have a right to live—art has always been a vital dimension. Aesthetics, ethics, and politics are three fields that have been addressed by philosophers from antiquity until today. But somehow when it comes to the pursuit of knowledge and education, aesthetics doesn't receive the same level of support as other fields. Despite the recognition of the importance of the achievements in our field, it's always difficult to procure financial support. Considering this problem, I think we are doing quite well. However, with very poor support coming from the government and federal agencies, the daily task of addressing this issue has now been added to our workload. Therefore, it's not easy to maintain the intensity of focus that we like to have here at MIT. The history of the Center for Advanced Visual Studies testifies to the complexity and weight of this problem. Over the years, we have had great moments and weak moments. It's an ongoing struggle. It is not enough that we are making art here and integrating art with knowledge. We also have to work as promoters and pedagogues who educate the administration and politicians about the importance of supporting us.

Interviewed 11/1/06

RODNEY BROOKS

Panasonic Professor of Robots
Director at MIT of Computer Science at the Artificial Intelligence Lab (until June 2007)

What are you working on here at MIT?

I work on developing robots. I began by working on mobile robots, then spent about two decades working on humanoid robots, and now I'm really interested in personal robots. Personal robots will empower people to increase productivity and, ultimately, become their own automation engineers. Basically, any person in a home or small business will be able to use a personal robot to help them do their work. Right now, robots like the ones we see in factories are dangerous. They can kill you unintentionally. So rather than developing more robots for these same types of big industrial tasks, I'm working on ones that can interact safely with people in ordinary spaces.

If you look back 25 or 30 years, computers were in backrooms. Regular people didn't interact with them. The people who oversaw these machines functioned as mysterious and mandatory go-betweens, akin to the way the priesthood has served as the medium between the congregation and the divine. Then came a tremendous liberation that allowed everyday people to use computers for all sorts of things—like e-mail and the Web—that even the original designers had never envisioned. I would like to empower people with mechanized physical action in the same way that we're currently being empowered with new actions for communication and computation.

A big breakthrough with personal computers occurred when office workers were suddenly able to program spreadsheets. They didn't consciously think about programming, they just looked at the screen and entered the numbers. Now I want people to be able to show a robot what they want done, and have it execute the task for them. I want them to talk to it, but not through a user's menu. The machines have to be completely interactive and give direct and useful feedback.

The major technical difficulty in this field is making the robots dexterous enough to touch and feel things, and also understand what those objects are. My goal is to build these machines with the visual recognition capabilities of a two-year old child and the manual dexterity of a six-year old child. Two-year olds can name all the objects in a room regardless or whether or not they were previously familiar with that environment. Six-year olds can tie their laces and accomplish all the manual tasks we require of

our robots.

Have there been any changes in your field in the recent past that have affected your research today?

When I first started building mobile robots, there were really only a few of them in the whole world. So I had to build everything by hand. In the 80's and early 90's, a lot of companies started building research mobile robots. Right now however, except for robots that are currently operated in factories, you can't buy a research robot that has a manipulator and a hand and arm. So if an independent researcher wanted to use one, he would have to build the hands and arms himself. Not many people in the world can do that. Lately though, there have been changes in certain technologies—like advances in processors and networks—that make things a lot easier than they used to be. I hope that nanotechnology will lead to the building of richly sensored hands. Human hands have so many different sorts of sensors, but the robot hands we build today have just a few sensors. As a result, they don't have any of the richness and nuance of touch and feel that we have.

Where do you see your research in the global context and where do you see your work going?

The demographics of the world are going to change drastically in the next 50 years. The birthrate is dropping in Europe, North America, Japan, Korea, and Taiwan. Those countries are also experiencing dramatic changes in the ratio of the working population versus the elderly, or retired, population. We will have to be more productive because there simply won't be enough working people to perform all the manual service jobs that must be done. I see a real opportunity for robots to help with that. Plus, I'm trying to go after some of those applications now because as I get older, (laugh) I'm going to want one.

What are the implications of your work? Is there a downside to what you're doing?

I see a lot of positives in what I'm doing. I wouldn't be doing it if I didn't. The negatives would be if society didn't want the help these robots can provide. It's very hard to predict these things. Look how the digital revolution has made its way all around the globe. I was in India a month ago and saw very poor people with very modest jobs pulling out cell phones on the side of the road, enjoying modern communication. So it's hard to say where it's all going to end up. I don't predict anything too ugly though. I don't foresee enslavement by machines. On the other hand, one should never underestimate people's capacity for evil.

Interviewed 3/7/06

ERIK D. DEMAINE

Esther and Harold Edgerton Professor
Associate Professor of Electrical Engineering and Computer Science

What are you working on here at MIT?

My work is in theoretical computer science. This field is essentially where computer science and mathematics meet. However, I consider myself more of a mathematician than an engineer. Within that framework, my focus is on algorithms. Basically, algorithms are the mathematical study of computer programs. We analyze what computers can do. For instance, there are some problems that cannot be solved efficiently. Other problems can't be solved at all by any program. Understanding what computers can and can't do is what we do as algorithmicists.

I work quite a bit with geometry. That means getting computers to solve geometry problems like paper folding, or robotic arm folding, or, ideally, protein folding. We also work a lot with data structures—that is, organizing data so you can search through it, or answer various questions about it, efficiently. Google is a really big data structure. In this structure, you want to be able to search for keywords, find documents that contain all of these keywords, and then rank them. We also work with graph algorithms and network algorithms. In this case, you answer basic questions about a network—for example, where to put the fire stations in a city in order to minimize the damage in a worst-case scenario, or determining the average time it takes for a fire truck to get to a random location.

Those are my main fields of study, but there are other things I do just for fun. I'm interested in what I call recreational algorithms, which are named after a field called recreational mathematics. Martin Gardner is more or less the father of recreational math and he's been a big influence on my dad (Martin Demaine) and me. So, we just study questions for play. For instance, can a computer play a game like Tetris? It turns out that it can, but not very well. Also, how does one design an algorithm to make art, or sculpture, or architecture? This might not be quite as serious as other things, but to me everything has the same motivation. They are interesting problems and fun to look at.

Many people are motivated to solve problems because they think they can change the world in a very direct way. In other words, a problem arises and someone wants to solve that problem, exactly that problem, so they can directly impact that particular domain. Some of the things I work on fall into that category, but that's not why I'm interested in

them. I'm interested in things for their own sake. When I see a problem that's dying to be answered, I want to find that answer, one way or the other.

That's one of the great things about mathematics. You always have an ultimate truth. Assuming you do mathematics correctly, and you write a proof carefully, you really can produce the answer to a question. It can never be refuted. Whereas in any other field, let's say in physics, you can have a hypothesis, and you can build evidence for that hypothesis, but you never really know for sure. Even if you did all the experiments correctly, it still doesn't prove the hypothesis. It only says that those experiments are consistent with that hypothesis. In math, you can actually prove something and know you have the answer.

What changes in and around your field affect your research today?

The academic world tends to move at a relatively slow pace, but I suppose it's all relative. Computers are changing. That influences us. Mathematics doesn't change very quickly, but it is changing all the time. Theoretical computer science is a very trendy field. These trends last about a year or two and then they fade away. People still work on them, but by then something else has taken off. I tend not to follow the trends. I like to work off the beaten path. I like to work on things that most people aren't working on. It's more interesting. I've always been that way. I used to not eat chocolate because it was too popular.

Recently, there has been more collaboration in the field. More and more people are working together in bigger groups. Traditionally, that hasn't been the case. The common model has been for someone to work in isolation and then present the results. Collaboration is now increasing in traditional mathematics, but theoretical computer science has definitely been pushing the envelope in this area. I'm part of this generation where collaboration is a normal thing. One of my first papers had twelve people on it. That is unheard of in mathematics. In physics it's a different story, but in mathematics twelve is a big number. I like to encourage people to work together more. For one thing, it makes research a lot more fun. It's very rare that I write a paper by myself, because it's not as interesting to me. With multiple people there's a social aspect, you get to chat and eat dinner and get to know one another while you're working. Also, I find it more productive. Each person brings a different set of tools to the table. Therefore, they combine to solve bigger problems than they could individually. I could never have done as much work as I have without my 174 collaborators, at last count. That makes a big difference in my life. I don't know exactly what has caused the change. Maybe it's because of e-mail. Maybe it's because plane travel has become more affordable. Perhaps it's just a change in attitude, but it's certainly a nice change.

Where do you see your work in a global context? Where do you see it going in the future?

Theoretical computer science has a track record of having a big impact in the world. I have not directly been a part of it, but it happens, and a lot of the time it happens by accident. And I think that's been the story of mathematics. People have gone off and studied some weird field for a long time and then at some point, oops, it has applications. In some sense, you could say the whole field of algorithms started out as just a hypothetical question. If we had computers, what things could we solve? As a result, people have found ways to answer all sorts of different problems which weren't practically solvable in the past, but are now.   In the long term, this has clearly had an impact on the world. Some of the major success stories are areas like cryptography. We can now do banking on the web because theoretical computer scientists came up with ways to send information so that it's protected.   But changing the world is not something I particularly look for. The hope is that it will happen, because it's nice to change the world, but in the fields of mathematics it's hard to predict what will have that power.

What are the implications of your work?

The Internet is all about anarchy. The U.S. tried to forbid cryptography for years. They tried to make it proprietary and they tried to make sure there was a back door so they could read all the messages that came in. But there's just no way to control the Internet. Even if you make something illegal, it still happens. Computers make the squelching of freedom of information impossible. Information is to be shared. If people are interested, if people want it, computers make it possible, and there's no stopping it. There are many projects underway to make the Internet more anonymous. As a result, people can do illegal things without repercussions. Now, I don't necessarily support law breaking, but it does force us to examine the laws themselves. And it raises the question, if there's no way to enforce the laws, then why are they there?

But I live in my little insular mathematical world. I study things that are intrinsically and aesthetically interesting to me. There are good things that come out of it and bad. But no matter what the repercussions of practical implementation are, we can at least say that we better understand things. There is intrinsic value in advancing the frontiers of science. Irrespective of the short-term implications, that is a positive impact on the world.

Interviewed 11/13/05

H. SEBASTIAN SEUNG

Professor of Computational Neuroscience
Investigator of the Howard Hughes Medical Institute

What are you working on here at MIT?

I work on the theory of neural networks. In my field, we are trying to understand how all mental phenomena arise from the brain. Specifically, we want to understand this in terms of interactions between single neurons. It is basically a reductionist approach. We are trying to explain brain function, from a microscopic point of view, as an outcome of interactions among a very large group of neurons inside the brain. It's analogous to physicists understanding properties of a piece of matter in terms of its atoms.

One thing we've been working on is the question of how humans and animals learn from experience. We are trying to formulate mathematical theories that explain how learning might take place through changes in the connections between neurons. The hypothesis is that each time you learn something based on reward or punishment, the synapses in your brain get changed. How does this happen? That's the question.

Another thing we are interested in these days, which is a departure for this lab, is the structure of the brain. We would like to know if it is possible to make a complete circuit diagram of the brain in the same way that you would for a computer. Let's say you wanted to understand a computer. You might look inside the computer, find every transistor, figure out how it is connected to other transistors, and make a huge list. We are part of a collaboration that wants to find new ways of doing that for human and animal brains.

What recent changes in and around your field have affected your work?

In the field of neuroscience, the big changes have occurred in our ability to measure things that could never be measured before—activity in certain areas of the brain, activity of neurons, concentrations of various chemicals, and now the microstructure of the brain. There are many different ways of looking at things. For instance, we can use the naked eye. If you dissected a brain you could actually see its structure. Of course, we can also look at it under a microscope and see an entirely new set of things that previously had been unrevealed. And now we can use an electron microscope that allows us to examine at an even higher resolution. We can see down to the level of single synapses and examine the connections between individual neurons. This enables us to visualize the

structure and function of the human brain. These are the big stories in neuroscience and they certainly have had a big influence.

Where do you see your work in a global context?

Well, in some sense, to understand the brain is to understand everything. Ultimately, all of the things we humans do are driven by brain function. So in this context, understanding the brain could be considered a theory about everything. We are still far from that goal, but it would help tremendously in our quest to better understand human behavior. We are our own worst enemies. Why can't we change all the terrible things that we do to ourselves and other people? Perhaps this knowledge would enable us to change human behavior. Additionally, this research should help us further develop artificial intelligence. We should be able to make machines that can do many of the same mental calculations and tasks as human beings. And we hope to, and should be able to, cure brain diseases. So there are quite a few large goals that we have.

Is there a downside?

Regarding my work, specifically, I am not sure that there is a downside. I suppose there is the question of whether too much knowledge about ourselves can somehow be bad. One can imagine that certain technological applications could be used to control and oppress people. It seems unlikely to me, but maybe that's because our research hasn't been as successful as research in other fields of science. When the physicists developed the atomic bomb, they had very clear proof of the practical applications of that knowledge. Progress in neuroscience has been much more difficult and abstract. So we tend to focus more on making advances than the potential downsides.

Interviewed 12/14/05

ANGELA BELCHER

**Germehausen Professor of Materials Science and Engineering
and Biological Engineering**

What are you working on here at MIT?

We try to understand how organisms make materials and expand those processes to materials that those organisms haven't had the opportunity to work with yet. We've been borrowing ideas from how abalone grow shells. About 500 million years ago in the ocean, abalone encountered changes in their environment such as increased calcium and other kinds of atoms. They had to learn how to process those changes and, in so doing, they built shells. They built calcium carbonate and silica. We want to do the same thing, but we want to self-assemble devices. So, we've been working with benign microorganisms to get them to display random peptide sequences on their surface. Instead of the 50 million years it took for these organisms to learn how to make shells, we want to have them learn how to make things in a really short period of time, such as days or weeks.

Right now we're primarily interested in electronics, energy, and medicine. One of our most recent projects has been focusing on how to get organisms, in this case a bacterial virus, to make electrodes for batteries. That's the project I've been working on with Paula Hammond and Yet-Ming Chiang. We've been engineering these bacterial viruses to grow cobalt oxide based materials and self-assemble onto an electrolyte to serve as a thin, flexible, lithium ion rechargeable battery.

What can that be used for?

For anything you could use a lithium ion battery for, but ours are going to be very, very thin, and they're going to be flexible and transparent. Basically, they'll look like Saran Wrap. So you could actually integrate them with clothing. You can think about them being transparent in your iPod or cell phone for instance, instead of having an additional thick battery.

And do you farm these viruses?

It is a farm, yes. Viruses can't make copies of themselves, so we keep making copies of them. They can't manufacture the atoms, so we have to pour the atoms in. They grab them out of the solution and start building them up to make the structures. One of the nice

things is that our process doesn't use any organic solvents at all. So, it uses the same conditions the biology lives in. It uses no high temperature. It uses room temperature. Basically, you can just dip-coat and make a battery on your benchtop. Another thing we're interested in is the fact that batteries currently have about 50% wasted mass. This mass is not actually used in the battery process itself, so we're trying to get rid of the excess material and just have active ingredients. So our processes are cheaper, greener, smaller, and thinner.

Are batteries your main focus now?

We don't really have a main focus. We focus on getting organisms to make materials.

And then the applications present themselves?

Yes. We've worked on electronics. We work on solar cells and fuel cells. We work on defect detection—that is, looking for defects on anything from airplane wings to semiconductors. And we're working on medical diagnostics, such as cancer detection.

Have there been any changes in the recent past that affect your research today?

Well, there have been some changes on the funding side. Funding for research in the United States has changed in that there is now much greater emphasis on the application. In the first couple of years it was more about the straight science, just working out the principles of how to control materials. But now we have to actually have relatively short-term applications.

This is very interdisciplinary research. In my group, there are students and post-docs from at least nine fields, all working together. When I was a graduate student, I was trained for my PhD among a physicist, a molecular biologist, and a chemist. So I was in early on the idea of interdisciplinary research. Now it's much more common, and that's fun to see. When I first got my PhD, I went from a degree that was basically in biology, to try to get a PhD in inorganic chemistry, and it just wasn't done. I had a hard time convincing them that I could do it. Now, students can get a degree in materials science, then go and get another degree in biology, and vice versa. That is encouraged. It is really, really nice, and it is much more accepted, which is great.

What role do you see your work playing in a global context and where do you see it going?

In terms of the global context, it has always been a focus of my group to try to make materials that are environmentally friendly, and process materials in a way that is not deleterious to the environment. If you look at how organisms process materials, they take materials from the environment—like abalone take calcium—but they don't add toxins back into their environment. So, we are interested in learning if the same processes can be used in the making of batteries, or fuel cells, or solar cells. That is definitely a global context.

We're interested in this process from an intellectual point of view, but we're always looking at the technology we develop to see how we can aid in specific areas. That is why we focus, and will stay focused, on energy and medicine. Another thing I'm very interested in is infection control. How can we, as people who travel all over the world, detect an infection and control it? Another really important area to be in is water, but we haven't really begun yet in that area.

These are all things I am very interested in. Let's focus on the infection control first. Would it be some kind of vaccine-based approach?

It is a function of tying up the infection and preventing the organisms from being able to infect. We have interest in vaccines, and we have interest in vaccine storage, but that is actually a different project. We aren't experts in this field, but we do think it is an area in which we can contribute. We're interested in the question of how to increase the stability of molecules that aren't normally stable at room temperature so they can be shipped to places that don't have refrigeration. It is a kind of infection control, but we're also interested in how you can inactivate viruses or infectious agents. We're looking at how you could, basically, wipe a surface and actually see infectious material. At the same time, wouldn't it be great if anything you picked up, you could prevent from infecting? Again though, I want to emphasize that I'm not an expert in this.

When I hear that viruses are grown, I'm thinking that they are going through some kind of evolution. Can the virus change and become problematic for humanity? Do you foresee a problem in that area?

Not with the kind of viruses that we're working with. We're working on bacterial viruses which are so far removed from any kind of mammalian or human virus that the possibility of them having a negative effect on humans is zero. It is not going to happen.

But can they interfere with whatever environment they're in?

They are very stable. They've been studied for a long, long time and have been used in biomedical applications for fifty years. We actually add extra genes into them to get them to grow materials. The only mutations we've ever seen are when they kick those genes back and return to their original selves.

How is your group approaching water issues?

As I said, right now it is hard to think about how we could get into water except for some ideas on water purification, but that would be on a small scale. It would be interesting to figure out how to get into large-scale water purification. We are always asking ourselves how we can apply our technology to help solve a problem. We are now working on using sunlight to convert water to hydrogen and oxygen for fuel cells.

What are the implications of the work? Are there limitations or a downside?

Well, I am surprised how far we've been able to push the technology and how we've been able to basically manipulate proteins to grow many kinds of structures that you wouldn't expect them to be able to grow. We'll run into limits, but I'm not sure what those are yet. We make materials as prototypes. Thinking about a process by which all batteries could be based on biological components is nothing trivial. Another thing is that some of the fields that we've picked are fields that are extremely competitive. They are also fields where the margin of profit may be very narrow. We can't just throw out how things are currently made and say, "Okay, now we're going to make batteries using self-assembled biology." I've always thought one of the most interesting aspects of our research is that it is focused on more environmentally friendly processing. But if it isn't cheaper, then companies aren't going to be interested. It has to be cheaper, better, and environmentally friendly.

Interviewed 4/11/06

PAULA T. HAMMOND

Professor of Chemical Engineering

What are you working on here at MIT?

I work in the area of self-assembly of polymers. One the one hand, we look at two-dimensional self-assembly, in which we are putting together polymers using charge attractions to create films that are assembled from a surface and structured on the nanometer length scale. In this case, we have a number of interesting material systems that can contain different functionalities, and the applications range from energy and electrochemistry, to biomaterials and drug delivery. In this 2-D area, we have also done a range of micro-scale and nano-scale patterning of these kinds of thin films.

On the other hand, we also look at three-dimensional self-assembly. In this case, we look at polymers which undergo a thermodynamically driven assembly to create nano-scale structures in 3-D. Some of the most interesting things we've been looking at more recently involve the creation of materials which assemble in solution into nanoparticles which can be used as carriers for drugs or as nano-scale structures that can serve as a template for other materials.

Could you, in layman's terms, explain how you might do that patterning, and then maybe talk about one specific project?

Sure. Perhaps 60% of my group works with the layer-by-layer thin film assembly approach. We're using electrostatics to build up a functional polymer thin film, one layer at a time. Each layer has dimensions ranging from molecular to tens of nanometers in scale. You can take a substrate with some initial charge, and dip it into a bath that contains a dilute solution of a polymer which contains the opposite charge. That polymer will be attracted to the charge on the surface and absorb to the substrate until, finally, the surface charge is reversed. Because the polymers in solution now have the same charge as the surface, electrostatic repulsion prevents further deposition. The amount that is absorbed depends on the charge density along the polymer chain, which can be changed to get a desired thickness. If acid or basic amine groups are present on the polymer chain, changes in pH will increase or decrease the charge along the polymer backbone. You can also add salt to the solution, which shields the charge along the backbone and makes it act as if it has less charge. In either case, you end up either with something

that is absorbed very flatly on the charged surface, or polymers that are adsorbed to the surface in thick loopy coils, akin to a shag carpet on the surface. Adsorption, by the way, is when the material just sticks to the top of the surface of a substrate. Absorption is when it goes into the bulk material, like water into a sponge. The thicknesses of those layers can range from five angstroms, which is half a nanometer, to tens of nanometers. After the polymer adsorption step, we rinse the substrate in dilute water to remove anything that isn't truly absorbed, and then adsorb another polymer of opposite charge. In this manner, by alternating the adsorption of oppositely charged polymers, we continue to build up this material system layer by layer.

The nice thing about this approach is that you can vary what goes into the thin film at different points along the thickness of the film. That is how we can build up entire devices using basically a couple of beakers, water, and charged polymers. We can build up materials that are conducting at an electrode surface, and then introduce polymers that undergo the color change we want for a display. We can introduce different materials that can undergo different types of color changes.

The electrochromic area is fun because I like optical effects and color. We do a lot of work with the incorporation of charged nanocrystals with polymers in this electrochromic area. We have, for example, a system in which we have a nanocrystal that undergoes a clear to blue transition, and a polymer that undergoes a green to yellow change. When the two systems are layered together within a thin film device, at different applied fields, we can get first a blue layer, then a green, and then a yellow one at different potentials, all by creating this sandwiched layer. These polymer chains essentially talk to each other as well, so you can get synergistic interactions between polymers, which happens in some of our electrochromic films, and they can also introduce some interesting phenomena.

In this electrochromic material system, we have a negatively charged particle that we can introduce into the layers. The particle has three oxidation states. Each oxidation state is a different color, but at the last oxidation state, all of the charge on the particle is lost entirely. If the film is in water and you lose the charge of the particle, the material begins to dissolve away, because the positively charged polymer that was layered with the particle is repulsed by its own charge. We can then electroc hemically control how much of the film dissolves. We actually wondered whether we could take this electrochemical behavior and turn it into a drug delivery approach, where we use electrochemistry to deliver drugs. First, we checked to see if the particle is toxic. It is not. Prussian blue has actually been used as a therapeutic for mercury poisoning, and it is completely nontoxic. Therefore, we can actually build up these films, with a drug in these multiple layers, and we can release the drug by applying a potential. We can hold it still by stopping the potential, and we can release more of the drug by applying it. This has very interesting ramifications for biomedical devices.

The fact that we can actually apply these thin films, build them up on a polysilicone stamp that has micron-sized features, and transfer the entire film onto any other substrate means that we could actually build up a drug chip where we have these different films in different places. And there is one more dimension to this, which is that we are able to introduce different drugs in different layers of the film. Ideally, they would be electrochemically sloughed off in order. This would be relevant, for example, for attacking a tumor in the brain. In that case, you can't do a systemic delivery through blood. You have to get through the blood-brain barrier. Generally, surgical procedures are still used, but you can insert something after that surgery that is going to electrochemically deliver these drugs at the right times. This method might also be used for delivering steroids or neurological drugs.

However, there are also situations in which you'd like something that isn't electrochemically stimulated, just something that releases continually over time, especially when you're talking about the surface of an implant or device. For example, a stent is the one everyone relates to, because drug coated stents have really changed that market. But stents only release one drug—you mix the drug in with a polymer, it releases, and you're done. What if you could release different drugs, at different times, at very controlled rates? In stents, you'd want to have a phase in which you promote healing, but also another phase in which you prevent blood clotting, growth of scar tissue, and other potential complications.

This is also interesting for orthopedic implants. In a hip implant replacement, for example, you want to remove infection in the bone first, then you want to deliver a drug that might promote cell healing and growth. It turns out that there are growth factors that do that. But it is often the case that you want one growth factor to come first, to help cells proliferate, and then at some point you want to stop the proliferation, so the cells can differentiate into the final phenotype, or form, that is going to be active. You can actually deliver a second growth factor specifically for that, and the ability to do it in a specific order makes a tremendous difference. So this is one of the areas where we're looking at this ability to control things, using this very simple all-aqueous approach, layer by layer. We can also deliver drugs layer by layer in reverse, by using a hydrolytically degradable polymer as one of the polymers that becomes incorporated.

This is one of the areas where we see an opportunity to approach a number of biomedical problems. One must always consider the push and pull of new discovery versus the need that is present in the marketplace. Here we have a perfect match. So, as a first approach, we've actually been talking to orthopedic surgeons, and to a range of other people in the biomedical area, and it appears that this is interesting not only for orthopedic implants, but also for virtually anything that gets put in the body. These films are very thin, and they can be coated on any surface. We can even coat fibers, such as sutures, with these. This is a huge opportunity. The difference here is that more traditional polymer processing doesn't allow us to do this sequential drug delivery. Another difference is that, typically, polymers need solvents like toluene and chloroform, and, besides having residuals that we don't want to deal with, these are things that destroy the efficacy of very sensitive drugs. You might think of some of the newer biological drugs as proteins or antibodies which can denature quite easily. You can't heat them and you can't expose them to solvents without losing activity of the drug. But our method uses water, so we can use this all-aqueous process.

From my research on your work I saw that, in terms of working with fabrics or fibers, detection of chemical or biological agents was possible?

Using the layer-by-layer technique, we know that we can coat fabrics and fibers. One of the things that we are working on in the Institute for Soldier Nanotechnologies is actually incorporating nanoparticles which are reactive semiconductors. The films we create right now are highly reactive to chemical toxic agents, so we can make chemically reactive protective coatings. This is the kind of thing that would be the lining inside a uniform or jacket for chemical warfare. It would be lighter and more breathable than the currently used activated charcoal and rubber based linings of protective suits. Our materials, because they are polyelectrolytes, allow the transmission of water vapor, but can block out other gasses and can chemically react to and destroy toxic materials.

The next level, which is what we're beginning to work on now, is actually the incorporation of these systems so that we have semi-conducting particles that are in contact with each other and which can undergo an electrical response in the presence of small amounts of the chemical agent. So we are using some of the same chemistries, but the assembly happens with different levels of hierarchical order. We are interested in using the more traditional nanoparticles, but also, in our collaboration with the Belcher group, we think we can use viruses genetically engineered in her group as a way to generate biomineralized inorganic materials that would be useful for other electrochemical devices or sensors.

Do you envision that being used only in the military, or also in the general public?

This would be for the general public, law enforcement, emergency responders, firefighters—the whole range. We started by looking at chemical warfare agents, but are now beginning to look at carbon monoxide, nitrates and nitrites, ammonia, and things that might exist in a chemical or toxic environment. So it is becoming very relevant.

Have there been any considerable changes in the recent past that affect your research today?

One of the most obvious changes, both with respect to government funding and priority in the public consciousness, is the interest in attacking specific biomedical problems. My background is originally in the electro-chemical, electro-optical work. I'd say my core is in designing materials, synthesis, and polymer processing. When I first started, my applications were directed towards displays and things of this nature. But the first obvious change was the interest in biomedical problems, the manipulations of cells, and the development and understanding of the fact that materials have a huge impact in the way cells function and grow. So I ended up in collaboration with colleagues in fields such as biology and biological engineering, and with some of my material science friends who were interested in these problems. But people were dealing more with cellular behavior, and the realization in the biomedical field that materials can do a lot more than just sit there and act as a structural component has triggered interest from my community. Now we are looking at how we can use our chemical and materials approaches to do things like manipulate cells and deliver drugs.

The second big set of changes was in 2001. There was a broad agency announcement for an institute that would address soldier's needs. I became involved in that with my colleagues and we started to write a proposal. Then 9/11 happened, and the relevance of our research was sharpened incredibly, because material science can be used to protect not only soldiers, but also the general public. So now there was big interest in everything from sensing technologies and protective technologies, to material systems that might be responsive in other ways. Certainly, the ability to draw the Institute for Soldier Nanotechnology here to MIT was a significant development. It helped people in my community within the Institute to interact with each other and to become a part of the nationwide response to these problems that we see now.

Technologically, I think our ability to study things on the molecular and nanometer scale with more efficiency, more regularity, and more consistency has allowed us to better appreciate what is happening on that level. The atomic force microscope, for instance, had a huge impact on my work and everyone else's. The ability to see what is going on, to be able to probe it, and the ability to make nanomechanical measurements has had a huge effect. And that echoes throughout all of the forms of microscopy and spectroscopic techniques.

What role do you see your research playing in a global context and where do you see it going?

This is a really interesting question. On a global level, I see two areas which should have real impact. One is the biomedical area. We're looking at targeted drug delivery of cancer drugs, improved chemotherapy, improved delivery of drugs from implants, and new approaches to delivering drugs in general. But I also have another platform for our layer-by-layer work, which is closer to the sensors and the electro-chemistry and the electrochromics, but it has to do with energy. In using almost the same kinds of approaches, we are looking at the creation of ultra-thin films for fuel cells for highly lightweight and efficient batteries and photovoltaics that operate at low temperature. I think there are huge possibilities there. Electrochemical functionality in these thin films is going to lead us not only to sensing capabilities and to protection for the solider, but also to new power capabilities which will impact the world.

Is your work related in any way to solar energy?

We have work in photovoltaics. We have work in fuel cells, which could use a range of different fuels, so to speak. And, as I said, we're beginning to look at batteries.

Within what time frame do you foresee the implementation of these technologies?

I think the biomedical technology might be the one that moves most quickly, in part because of where we are in the work, and in part because of the availability of funding for that. In terms of energy, that area is improving, and I think we may be able to see impacts in five to ten years with thin film technologies that could be used on a regular basis. There is work going on in my lab, and in my colleagues' labs, which is producing really remarkable developments that will make accessibility to these kinds of energy resources much more routine. All we need now to implement them is global social pressure, but I think we're beginning to get that.

What are the implications of the implementation of your work? Is there a downside?

The technology of this layer-by-layer technique, in terms of processing and materials usage, is actually an improvement over the techniques we had before. This is because of the aqueous solution processing and the fact that many of the polymers can be selected to be natural polymers, including, in some cases, polypeptides. As far as a negative impact—I'm thinking carefully about this—I think the area in need of most thought is materials systems that are used to protect the soldiers and the first responders. That is clearly a positive application, but in the wrong hands those same technologies could be used aggressively. What we have to be careful of, as a society, is that we don't say, "Well, now that we're protected from this stuff, let's just use it." I don't necessarily feel that is the direction we're going in, but it certainly has come up in conversations with some colleagues. In fact, when I did a fellowship at Radcliffe during my sabbatical, that was what some of my artist and social science colleagues were concerned about. When we enable ourselves to survive, we must also enable others to survive, and we must make sure that we don't use this as a reason to more freely engage in unnecessary force. It should be used as a protective measure when needed to keep the peace.

That requires a great deal of responsibility and restraint.

I agree. There are similar concerns in any kind of DNA field.   We must cultivate not only the ability to manipulate, but also the ethics of implementation.

Do you see any real danger in the medical field? Do you see any possibilities for genetic alteration?

The projects where we are delivering growth factors are pretty innocuous, but there are projects where we deliver genes for gene therapy, which can, for example, be designed to be suicide genes that cause a cancer cell to kill itself. The problem is that this technology not only enables us to attack disease, but also can be designed to enable alteration of the function of tissues and organs. How do we regulate this and make sure this research is about curing disease and not about altering something that is natural? I definitely feel very protective about those aspects of the work. Clearly, in those areas, extreme ethical thought must take place.

Interviewed 4/5/06

DARRELL IRVINE

Eugene Bell Associate Professor of Tissue Engineering

What are you working on here at MIT?

In our lab, we work at the interface of the physical sciences and life sciences. My own graduate training was in polymeric materials physics/chemistry. Then in my post-doctoral work, I moved into the life sciences field of immunology. What we do here is bring those two areas together. We try to use new kinds of materials as a way to either study immunology, study how immune cells work, or make new types of therapies.

We focus on the biology of how immune responses work. Then, by building on what we know about the cell and molecular biology of the immune system, we try to design rational, safe vaccines. For example, we're putting a lot of effort into making materials that, when injected as a vaccine, can mimic the cascade of events that happen during a natural infection. Our immune systems are evolutionarily engineered to respond very rapidly and robustly. We're creating vaccines that can do that, and are simultaneously safe and easy to manufacture. That's one of the main focuses of the lab.

Can you discuss a particular vaccine project you are working on?

In the work where we've made the most headway, we haven't focused on a particular disease at the start. Because there are a lot of things we believe would be characteristic of any good vaccine, or that would be characteristic of a class of vaccines, we begin with a more general study. Many of the infections that we don't have good vaccines for—such as HIV, Hepatitis C, malaria, and so on—have certain common traits. For instance, we think that a good vaccine would have to elicit both potent CD8 T-cell and antibody-based immunity. So we began by asking how we could make a vaccine that can potently stimulate both arms of the immune response—the T-cell and the B-cell side of the immune response—to give that kind of protection.

In one case, we began by examining how in a natural infection, infected cells actually, as a defense mechanism, secrete molecules that attract immune cells to the site of the infected tissue. That's a way to quickly spread the alarm and concentrate the cells you need where you need them. So, we've been looking at the possibility of using synthetic materials that could be injected and not only deliver the antigen that starts the immune

response, but also release proteins called chemokines, which will attract the immune system to that location and take these very rare immune cells that are spread out looking for an infection and drive them to the place where they're needed.

Have there been any considerable changes in and around your field in the recent past that affect your research today?

Over the last three years, we have seen the advent of a new method of visualizing immune responses in small animals. The process is called two-photon microscopy. By labeling cells and actually watching them move within tissues, we can observe how immune responses are occurring. This has really changed how the field of immunology works, and has changed the way we think about experiments, because it has altered our parameters for understanding what we're trying to engineer. With the tools we now have available, we can actually think of visualizing what's going on at an immunization site, instead of just injecting and hoping for the best.

On another scale, something that has changed in recent years, but really hasn't affected what I'm doing personally, is the growing concern about biowarfare agents, or pathogens, that could be part of a terrorist attack. The government is supporting a lot of research aimed at developing vaccines for things like anthrax, and what they call class C pathogens. That has shifted the direction of a lot of people's research. Because we, in our group, don't really have an infectious disease background, we haven't gone in that direction.

What role do you think your work is playing in a global context and where do you see it going?

Certainly, we're very conscious of the fact that the largest population in need of vaccines is in developing countries. That is something we are thinking about all the time. In addition to making a vaccine that works, you'd like to create one that can withstand shipping, be shipped without cold storage, and be inexpensive. If we were to succeed in creating an HIV vaccine, those concerns would obviously be of paramount importance. A $10,000 vaccine will not be of use.

Furthermore, people in developing countries often have continuous, multiple infections. This actually alters the way the immune system is able to respond to a new infection or a new vaccine, and can sometimes dampen its response. So it is possible that vaccines which work in the First World, might be completely ineffective in developing countries. Therefore, a vaccine sometimes has to be consciously designed for a specific application.

What are the implications of your work? Is there a downside?

We're not working on, say, viral vector-based vaccines, where there are concerns that viral vectors could integrate with host cells and create the potential for possible side effects, such as cancer. That's one of the motivating reasons why we're working on these entirely nonliving, synthetic systems. However, these synthetic, nonliving vaccines may have their own issues that remain to be discovered.

I understand that viruses are very good at mutating in order to become more complex and resistant. And sometimes, as with genetically manipulated food, big problems may arise later, and then technology has to catch up again. Is that something you're worried about?

Are we worried that by working on certain vaccines, we might aid the evolution of pathogens?

Yes.

Well, to be frank, I think this is very difficult to say, but I would doubt it. In the case of HIV, the virus in its current state is such an adept mutator that it's unlikely we'd do anything in the course of pursuing treatment that would make it more mutable. It's already mutating at a rate that's approaching the limit of how any structure could mutate and still remain functional.

So you are thinking about a vaccine for HIV?

We're beginning to. In terms of prophylactic vaccination, HIV is such a difficult problem that, at first, I didn't want to get into that arena. But because it is such a compelling problem, we're starting to think about it, albeit on a very basic level. We're now beginning to think about whether the synthetic materials that we make for vaccines could be used to make oral vaccines. If so, you would just take a pill and be vaccinated. That would help with compliance and distribution in developing countries. But also, for an infection like HIV that goes into the mucosal regions, the immunity that you would generate in the gut would be the right kind of immunity to prevent against a first infection.

Regarding possible dangers, I think the only thing that really concerns people is when we try to drive the immune system to do something beyond what it is capable of doing on its own. An example is cancer therapy. People would like to make cancer vaccines too. There, the challenge is really a race between growth of a tumor and expansion of immune cells to fight the tumor. Right now, people are trying to win that battle by, say, transferring enormous numbers of activated T-cells into patients. In one therapy, called adoptive transfer therapy, you begin with a tumor biopsy. In such a biopsy, one can actually see that some T-cells have infiltrated, but have been shut down by the tumor. So, you recover the inactive T-cells, activate them in the laboratory, and then expand them and re-infuse them into the patient in the hope of fighting the tumor. One concern when you're doing this type of great expansion of these highly regulated cells is the side effect of autoimmunity, because you might activate cells that also have an affinity for self-antigens. There is evidence that this can happen. Now, whether or not it's really a serious concern is not clear yet, because if a patient gets Vitiligo but is cured from cancer, no one is going to care. In general though, that is a main concern. When we find solutions to these problems, are they simply going to introduce other problems? It's not completely known. We're just beginning to understand well enough how the immune system works to even start thinking about those questions.

Interviewed 4/3/06

SCOTT R. MANALIS

Associate Professor of Biological and Mechanical Engineering

What are you working on here at MIT?

We're working on using silicon technology—that is, all of the techniques that are used to make integrated circuits—to make new measurement methods for biology. Essentially, we have expertise in microfluidics and we develop new ways to measure the parameters that are relevant to living systems. This can be used in diagnostics or to better understand biological processes. In many cases, we exploit the unique physical properties associated with micro and nanoscale dimensions to make measurements that are faster, better, and more sensitive than what is possible with existing methods.

Can you be more specific?

Sure. In terms of the motivation and the bigger picture, let's consider a computer room from the 1950's. Have you ever seen pictures of those computers from the 50's? They're big, and there were just a few people who knew how to use them. If you wanted to process information back then, you didn't do it on your desktop. You would send it over to experienced users and they would take it from there.

If you go to a biology lab today, in many ways it looks similar to that. Let's say you have a certain protein that's related to a signature for breast cancer and you want to have it measured. Your doctor would send it to a centralized lab, wait a few days, and then get it back. In the world of computers, everything changed with the invention of the integrated circuit. With the invention of the transistor, and the ability to make integrated circuits, all of a sudden what could previously only be done in that computer room could now happen instantly on a chip. Subsequently, those chips were then used in ways that had never been previously considered. They went into microwave ovens, cell phones, toys—everywhere. That critical revolution is starting to take place in terms of the way biological measurements are made.

My lab works within a field that is making this happen. The goal is to make a lab-on-a-chip, and this requires that a lot of different components are integrated to work together. When you take a sample of your blood and have something measured in it, there are many processing steps that must take place before you get the result. Right now, all

these steps take place on different parts of the benchtop. Users or robots with a pipette will take something here and move it over there. That's very tedious. It also requires quite a large sample volume, because when you pipette, it requires a certain amount of fluid. Now if the process were miniaturized, less sample would be required. And if it were integrated and automated, it would be much faster. The goal is to do that in a way that is programmable and general to many different measurements. In the computer world, this would be equivalent to the idea of developing software independently of the industries that are developing the microelectronics. This is what has made microprocessors so successful. The same could ultimately be true here. Someone would be able to think, "Okay, I want to use a lab-on-a-chip to measure several different biomarkers for prostate cancer." Then they would write a set of code to determine how the chip should be controlled in different areas, and it would do that. Of course, someone else could do something completely different with a different code, but it would still be the same hardware.

Have there been any changes in your field in the recent past, or in general, that affect your research today?

Much of my research is enabled by the techniques that are used to process silicon. Many of the techniques for developing a lab-on-a-chip have been enabled by processes for integrated circuits and advances in the semiconductor industry. I'd say that is probably the single most important thing that is allowing my lab to make what we make. Do you want to see something that we've made? Have you seen these sorts of things before?

I have not.

Here is a chip. It has holes that go partway through it. That is where fluids come in. The fluids are then directed to areas where very tiny amounts are measured. These chips are made on wafers that are much larger than this—the size of pizzas—but then they're replicated and made a hundred times over. If these things could measure and then tell you something interesting about your health, and they could be made for a few dollars a piece, then they could be distributed to a large number of people and used to make predictive measurements about disease. That's one reason why this technology is so interesting. The devices achieve extremely high sensitivity and they are completely mass-producible.

What role do you see your work playing in a global context and where would you like to see it go?

Work in my lab, and from others in the field, could lead to low-cost diagnostics that are cheap and robust. For example, there is an increasing demand for HIV diagnostics that enumerate CD4 cells and measure viral load. Unfortunately, the existing ones are often too costly for people in many parts of the world. Microfluidic-based technologies could change this.

What are the implications of the implementation of your work? Do you see a downside?

Our focus is on developing new technologies to advance the life sciences. You can always question certain approaches and how particular resources are allocated, but it would be hard to find a true downside. Ultimately, all of this is aimed at making people healthier.

Interviewed 2/15/06

KIMBERLY HAMAD-SCHIFFERLI

Esther and Harold E. Assistant Professor of Mechanical Engineering and Biological Engineering

What are you working on here at MIT?

I'm working on a way to control biomolecules by using nanoparticles as antennas. If you think of a cell, it is a big, wet bag of proteins all mixed up together. Controlling the individual proteins in there is quite difficult. Our technique will allow us to effectively and easily switch biomolecules on and off. This binary approach will allow us to pinpoint which particular gene is causing a sickness. This will enable new methods for disease diagnosis and therapy. There has never been anything like this. It is a new area.

What diseases are you targeting?

We aren't targeting any diseases right now. We're still very much in the early stage. We're doing proof of principle systems, studying how it works. Then, eventually, we're going to work on using this technique to control disease.

What is the size of these antennas?

They have to be nanometer sized. They have to be the size of a protein so they can go inside a cell.

Have there been any considerable changes in your field that affect your research today?

That is an interesting question because I've jumped fields a lot. I was trained as a chemist. I started out in chemistry as an undergraduate here at MIT. Now, I've moved into mechanical and biological engineering. I would say that the fusion of engineering with biology has made this work possible. Prior to that synthesis between the disciplines, people didn't really think about how to engineer biological systems. Now scientists are trying to do that. This has happened very recently. If people hadn't begun thinking about things in this way, we wouldn't be where we are. We came along at the right time.

What role is your work playing in a global context and where do you see it going?

The fusion of nanotechnology with bioengineering is unprecedented. People have heard

about nanotechnology, but they're probably wondering how it is going to affect their lives. We already have nanoscale systems in clothing and hockey sticks, but we really don't yet know the implications for health care and medicine. If we can control these proteins through an external field, that would have serious implications for disease control.

In terms of diagnosis of disease, we really hope that this will be a very useful technique. But it is also interesting just as a new tool for biologists. Biology is a very hard system to study and there aren't a lot of good, precise tools out there. We hope our technique will help. Because it is universal, it could have ramifications for many areas of biological study. That's our end goal, but we're still a long way off.

Are there other applications? Could it be used in the environment?

You know, actually we haven't thought about that. We've thought mostly about organisms and humans, but haven't thought a lot about environmental systems. It could be, we just haven't thought about good model systems for that. The human system is very well studied and there are a lot of simple systems we can test, so that is what we've targeted. But eventually, yes, we could do that. It would be a lot of fun.

What are the limitations of the work? Is there a downside?

Yes, there is a downside, namely the negative health side effects of nanotechnology. FDA tests are just beginning. Environmental protection agencies are starting environmental tests on nanoparticles to see what happens when you put them in a person. They're beginning to see that it does very bad things.

Such as?

It can slow the growth of cells. It can affect mobility. It can affect the shape of cells. If it is in an organism, that is just the beginning. It could have some serious health implications.

Interviewed 3/20/06

ALICE Y. TING

Associate Professor of Chemistry

What are you working on here at MIT?

Using the tools and principles of chemistry, we develop enabling technologies that help biologists understand cell signaling. For example, the dream of every biologist would be to take any particular molecule of interest inside a cell—it could be one protein out of the 20,000 different proteins that are present—and examine its behavior during all types of different processes. These processes include but are not limited to cell division, the process by which a cell becomes cancerous, the process of cell death, and the process of differentiation. If we could essentially make a movie of this, with angstrom resolution and in real time, we could actually figure out how the protein functions, behaves, interacts with its neighbors, and moves around within the cell. Unfortunately, this is currently impossible. But in the big picture, we're trying to develop technologies that will make it possible. We're making methodologies that allow us to take various chemical probes, which are capable of reading out specific types of information about proteins, and target them to any specific molecule we're interested in learning about. So it's a chemical problem, but it has biological applications.

Could you mention a specific example?

When I'm telling non-scientists about the work we do, I typically show a movie. The nice thing about our research is that it's very visual. Let me give you a specific example. ABL is a protein, and when there is a mutation that causes the behavior to become irregular, a particular cancer called chronic myelogenous leukemia can arise. A recent drug, which is very successful at curing this particular form of cancer, is called Gleevec. It is sold by Novartis and it is one of the most successful examples of drug design. Its molecular target inside the patient is this protein called ABL. Because it is such an important drug target and is a link to this particular type of cancer, everyone would like to know what it does. What are its biological functions? How does it behave in a cell? Now, in traditional cell biology, the most common way to study proteins is to take, say, a million cells, kill them, and then extract and study the purified protein of interest in a test tube. But when you study a protein in its purified form, you're losing a tremendous amount of information due to the fact that it's no longer in its natural context. You're losing information about how it's trafficking inside the cell, you're losing information about how it's being regulated

by different cellular components, and you're losing single cell information because you're averaging across a large and heterogeneous population. So we developed a way to visualize, in a single live cell, exactly when ABL is activated. We can do this because it's an enzyme that shuttles between the active and the inactive form. Being able to visualize when it's on, when it's off, and where that happens, provides much more information than the traditional cell biological techniques.

In this movie (shows video clip), we've got a cell—this is just one cell at 40x magnification—in which we've introduced our special reporter molecule that we designed from scratch using chemistry. We introduced it everywhere inside the cell. This reporter molecule emits light, but it's the color of the light which reflects the information about how active ABL is. When the reporter detects that ABL is active, it emits red light. When it detects that it's not active, it emits blue light. And there are gradations in between. So everywhere you see red, there is high activation of the enzyme, and everywhere you see blue, there is low activity. In the nucleus of the cell you have low activity, and elsewhere you have higher activity.

During this experiment, I add a growth factor called platelet-derived growth factor, or PDGF. When this is added to cells, the ABL gets activated, but the special pattern of activation is what's interesting. Here, what you see is what happens when I add PDGF. There is an overall elevation of ABL activity in the cytoplasm and these membrane ruffles form. This happens when the membrane is bunching up and the cell is getting ready to migrate. Locally, within these membrane ruffles you have the highest ABL activity. This suggests that ABL is playing a role in forming these ruffles and is involved in cell migration.

That's one specific example of what we do. We start from the molecular level, do engineering, and then perform examinations in the cell biological context in order to gain insight into how a protein that is important in disease behaves.

What recent changes in your field have affected your research today?

My field is highly interdisciplinary. It would most accurately be called molecular imaging. Molecular imaging brings together biologists, chemists, and physicists. I'm coming at it from the angle of the chemist. I develop probes. We rely strongly on the expertise of biologists and physicists and the advances in those fields. Similarly, they depend on us.

There are many important things that are shaping the direction of our research. For example, in the world of physics, technologies for doing microscopy are getting better and better. There was a fantastic paper recently in PLoS Biology (Public Library of Science Biology). A German scientist named Winfried Denk developed a way to do electron microscopy in three dimensions. This is phenomenal. The majority of the work we do here is in optical microscopy. Electron microscopy offers an enormous advantage over optical microscopy in that you get vastly improved spatial resolution. Instead of being able to visualize things at 200 nm, you can see them at 5 nm. That means that with this technology, we can start visualizing cellular structures that are completely invisible to optical microscopy. Until now, there have been two big problems with electron microscopy: you couldn't do it on live cells—so you couldn't get that real time information, that movie we spoke of—and you couldn't see it in three dimensions. Now, one of these problems has been solved.

That type of advance influences my work because, suddenly, I realize that electron microscopy is becoming more powerful and potentially more useful for addressing biological problems. Now I want to shift my research and begin developing chemical probes that can be used for electron microscopy, not just optical microscopy. Amazing things are happening in biology all the time, interesting discoveries that open up a whole collection of new problems. And these new problems make me think, "What are the technological limitations to solving these problems and what can I contribute to help break down those barriers?"

Where do you see your work in a global context and where do you see it going?

Our type of science is fundamentally different from hypothesis-driven research that is focused on a specific problem. The traditional biologist says, "I'm interested in why a leaf grows towards the sun." He comes up with hypotheses and then spends his life testing them to figure out the molecular mechanisms that cause the leaf to grow the way it does. That is important work, but it's not the type of research we do. We come from the perspective of chemistry and engineering. We want to provide enabling technologies that will allow researchers around the world to address their problems with more efficiency and power, and to solve problems they previously could not begin to solve. We want to push the technological boundaries. For example, the PCR reaction (polymerase chain reaction) made it possible to amplify tiny amounts of DNA into larger quantities. This is a technological, not a fundamental biological, discovery. It was awarded the Nobel Prize. DNA sequencing was also awarded the Nobel Prize. There are many technological advances that contribute broadly to the entire scientific community and make it possible to do research that was previously impossible. Those are the types of contributions we hope to make.

What are the implications of your work? Is there a downside?

I don't think there is a downside. I believe that scientific discovery and truth are inherently good and that there really isn't any downside to understanding things better. But if I step back and try to look at the question as a layperson would, I realize there are areas of research that may raise moral and ethical issues—for instance, stem cell research or research into the ways particular toxins work. But my research is not in any of those controversial areas. I don't see anything problematic about the work we do.

I have a very positive attitude towards research in general. For example, in the 1970's, when people developed recombinant DNA technology, suddenly you could take the gene from a jellyfish and express it in a mouse. In that picture right there (points at a photograph), that's a mouse expressing a gene from a jellyfish. That's why it's glowing green. That type of thing freaked people out because they said, "This is ridiculous. These are organisms that nature never intended." Even when I see things like that, it doesn't bother me. The positive impact of these technologies has far outweighed the negative impacts. It's possible that there are people who can do damaging or immoral things with any scientific advance, but it's not something that I think about very often. Despite the concerns about recombinant DNA technology, everything turned out okay. It's incredibly important, it has propelled research, and we use it all the time. People haven't been cloning all these strange organisms and wreaking havoc by unleashing them on the world. The worst nightmares were never realized. I can't predict the future, but so far it has worked out.

As for the implications of my research, if we develop a technology that lets one lab in the world make a discovery that they never would have been able to make with the existing technologies, and that discovery leads to an improved understanding of some basic biological process—how we think, how we learn, how we form memories, how during neurodegenerative diseases these processes go wrong—then I will feel very satisfied. That's what I'm hoping for. It would be great if we could make a contribution to an improved understanding of any fundamental biological process, either directly through our own efforts, or indirectly through people who benefit from our research. I would be thrilled about that.

I also think a lot about not only the impact of our research, but also the impact of my role as an advisor to future generations of scientists. I spend a lot of time trying to train the students in my lab to be well-rounded, thoughtful, creative, original scientists. I don't want them just slaving away at the bench. I want them to be able to communicate about their research, to be able to think outside of the box, and to have a wide perspective on the field. I want them to be really great scientists. I hope that after they leave my lab, they go on to do wonderful, amazing things and, ultimately, train their own scientists. If that happens, I will be deeply satisfied.

Interviewed 12/13/05

BERNHARDT L. TROUT

Associate Professor of Chemical Engineering
Director of the Molecular Engineering Laboratory

What are you working on here at MIT?

Right now, my major focus is biotechnology and pharmaceuticals. Originally, my work and interest in environmental catalysis and developing new ways of reducing pollutants were the main reasons I came to MIT. Unfortunately, it ended up being difficult to get funding for that. That was 1998. But I had a natural inclination toward pharmaceuticals. In a sense, the environmental work has a degree of negativity inherent to it, because you're preventing things from happening. In the human health field, you are helping people.

I've also worked extensively on automotive catalysis. As we know, CO_2 is a major greenhouse gas. We in carbon management are working to prevent CO_2 emission. Since my arrival at MIT, I've been working on materials called clathrate hydrates, which trap gases—such as CO_2 or natural gas—or other components that are potential energy sources. This process also has the potential to sequester and separate CO_2 and other gases.

Can you be more specific?

My research, in the broad sense, is called molecular engineering. I try to understand materials, compounds, and processes at the molecular level. In so doing, we use fundamental theoretical approaches such as statistical mechanics and quantum mechanics. We call these ab initio, or first principles, methods. They are necessary for an understanding of molecules and how molecules add up to make an incredibly complex and diverse variety of systems. We start from that point—the microscopic level—and then we work up to questions such as the effect of CO_2 in the oceans or the presence of clathrate hydrates in the permafrost seabed. We investigate how we can use our knowledge of the very basic properties to help us move toward a more comprehensive global understanding.

And what have you found?

One thing we found is a new theoretical approach for understanding clathrate hydrates, leading to new descriptions of processes involving these materials, as well as new ways

of designing them. We've also found new approaches for hindering the formation of clathrate hydrates when their presence is unfavorable. Our current goal is to be able to get energy in the form of natural gas from these clathrate hydrates by replacing the natural gas with CO_2, leading to zero sum emission. That's what we're currently working on.

Even though, as you mentioned earlier, it seems like work in this field has a lot of negative implications, aren't there still positive results that help stem global warming?

Everyone in the field of environmental research is addressing problems associated with technology. We are trying to solve manmade problems with manmade solutions. No one is working on understanding nature as nature. It is all about how humans interact with their environment via technology. It is a double-edged sword. On one hand, we have terrific advances and a lot of energy to use as we so desire. On the other hand, by using so much of it, we are creating very significant problems. We are not even attempting to come to terms with the basic meaning of what we are trying to do with technology.

Have there been considerable changes in the recent past that have affected your research?

Scientifically speaking, there have been significant changes over the past eight years. Very sophisticated theoretical tools have been developed which allow us to understand these complex processes, and we here at MIT are contributing to that development.

How do you see your research in a global context? Where do you think it is going in the future?

The theoretical methodology is clearly global. People all over the world are working on this. On the practical side, in terms of the state of the environment and the use of energy, I believe the biggest issues are social rather than political. The real hurdle is getting society to understand what is at stake here. It's plain to me that we aren't influencing that debate, or even participating much in it. The main issue at MIT with energy and environmental research is that there is little funding, which leads to few opportunities. We need greater financial resources, and we must figure out not only where the money should come from, but also what should be done with it when it arrives. Traditionally, the big thing at MIT has been government funding. The problem is that it often ends up wasted or poorly controlled. I don't know how many billions of dollars are spent on energy research in the U.S. Is it twenty billion, thirty billion, fifty billion? The issue is how the money is spent. How should we address scientific funding? In my opinion, professors are spending more and more time trying to get funds, and less time thinking, doing research, and teaching.

Are there other limitations, or downsides, to your work?

One general risk, always, is that things might not work. That's an important element. You have to balance risks with the potential for success. For example, we're trying to understand crystallization—which is a big issue in pharmaceuticals—and we're trying to use that understanding to create a more rational design process. Any tablet or pill that you take is crystallized. They are made of little crystals. However, no one really understands how the crystallization process works. It's considered black art. Developing a better understanding will lead to better control. From our perspective, it's all about the upside. The only downside is that if it doesn't work, we've been working in vain.

Interviewed 9/12/06

C. ADAM SCHLOSSER

Research Scientist for the Joint Program on the Science and Policy of Global Change

What are you working on?

My general area of research is global hydrological and ecological systems and how they relate to global climate change. Specifically, my role here in the laboratory is to work with physical scientists, ecologists, energy research scientists, global policy researchers, and economists to put together what we call a global integrated systems model. As you would probably expect, it's hard to do an experiment on nature. We basically use computer models to do these sorts of investigations. My role has been to use computerized representations of hydrological and ecological systems and find ways to link those systems with the physical climate system, the atmosphere, and the global economy in an idealized, computerized environment.

I've been working with a senior faculty member in the economics department, and with a post-doctorate researcher, trying to see if we can actually find relationships between how climate changes and how people respond to those climate changes in terms of industrial and domestic energy consumption. We run scenarios of climate futures and examine how those integrated systems respond to what we think may happen to the global environment.

Recently, a Gallup poll surveyed people—Americans, I believe—about their greatest concerns. The top two were what you'd expect: the war in Iraq and the economy. The environment was way down the list. Global warming was not in the top five. The top concerns were all related to water availability, water quality, and the security of our water systems. Where is our water is going? How do we use it? Is it contaminated? Is it toxic? What can we do about these things? These topics are close to my heart.

Primarily, my background has been global hydrology. We use models and data to understand not only what nature does, but also how these global hydrological systems respond when we impose change on the global system. What can we do to potentially mitigate any adversities or scarcities in water supplies for the future? Of course there is concern regarding the water supply, but I'm also very concerned about how the global water cycle changes with climate change. Do the frequencies of droughts and floods change as climate changes?

Do they?

Given the data we have now, it's very hard to decipher what is natural environmental change and what actually has to do with what we are doing to our environment. The conventional wisdom in our field right now is that as the atmosphere warms, its capacity to hold water increases. Our projection is that we will see a greater number of extreme hydrological events, i.e. floods and droughts. However, from the data and the observations we take, it's very hard to say unequivocally that this is occurring right now. It is hard to find evidence in the historical database to show that the trends we are seeing are specifically linked to what we are doing to our environment.

I'm a member of a NASA science team. It's called the NASA Energy and Water Cycle Study. It's a group comprised of about six core scientists and we've recently funded about a dozen principle investigators. This is an effort to really delve into questions about not only the global energy cycle, but also global water cycle issues and climate change. Not surprisingly, because it's NASA , we're looking toward satellite technology. That is, innovations in how we observe the global system using satellites, but also in situ data—in situ, meaning that I'm sitting here with a bucket measuring the rain coming out of the sky. We're trying to find ways to integrate all of this data to get a picture that's bigger than just putting together the sum of its parts. This is something we've just begun, but it's pretty exciting. Given the fact that NASA has had tough times recently, it's good to know that they want to invest money into doing these things.

There's an enormous amount of data that comes out of satellites. For one principal investigator to try to make sense of everything is a Herculean task. We're really trying now to get everybody looking at the bigger picture. Of course, every individual has his or her expertise, but we need everyone marching together here, not just one scientist going in a particular direction. I have to tell you, it's a struggle, but I'd like to think we're off to a good start.

Can you tell me a bit about what you've found regarding major industry and its relationship with the water supply?

We've recently done a study which involved a collection of data obtained from a Chinese ministry. It basically described certain climate variables, or certain climate states. The basic idea was to do a multi-tiered regression analysis between temperature and relative humidity. These are the two fundamental climate variables. As I mentioned before, when the atmosphere is warmed it has a propensity to hold more water. We tracked changes in these climate variables and also examined how energy is consumed both in the domestic and non-domestic fronts.

We discovered a couple of interesting results in our analysis. We're still in the preliminary stages, but I can tell you that there was a significant sensitivity, or a significant relationship, between temperature and domestic energy use. Overall, the study indicates that we can actually measure, we can actually quantify, an empirical relationship between climate changes, or climate variations, and energy demands. It's those relationships that go into the wiring of that global model that we're developing here. It's called the Integrated Global Systems Model.

Can you extrapolate from this local data to predict larger consequences?

There is a need to do this. But it's very important for us to make sure that the regional study can be extrapolated. You only really learn something when you can obtain and examine real data. It's easy to put together a model and come up with constructs and relationships that you think hold true, but it really boils down to making real world observations and building your models from there. That's the thrust of our research. Most of my time has been spent linking hydrological and ecological models. Prior to my coming on board here, the global ecological model was probably on the cutting edge in terms of research capability, but the hydrological model was lagging a little bit. I came on board to help in that area. Now, we have a model that is arguably one of the most internally consistent global-scale land models that links both hydrological and ecological systems to not only look at just the natural interplay between hydrological and ecological systems, but also to begin to look at how changes in our land environment are going to actually affect the water cycle and the global carbon cycle. Of course, the global carbon cycle ultimately feeds back into the global warming issue.

What recent changes in and around your field are affecting your research today?

I would say the real advances in our field have been related to our technological capability to represent all of the relevant systems in the global environment in a computer model. We try to get as much detail as possible into the model, within the practical limits of how much computer power we have, what sorts of experiments we want to run, and how long we are willing to wait for those experiments to run their course. It's a very delicate balance between how much detail to put into the physics, the biology, the sociology, and the economy of our system, and how much spatial detail we want.

How does public opinion impact funding?

I go back to that Gallup poll. When I'm sitting with a neighbor, they often say that my work is really interesting, but I can sense that it's not a topic they wake up every morning worrying about.

Do you wake up every morning worrying about it?

I wouldn't be doing this if I didn't feel passionately about it, and I wouldn't be particularly focused on what I'm researching if I didn't think it was important.

Do you feel it is something to be concerned about?

Yes, I do. You know, everybody wants to live as happily and as well as they can and enjoy all the comforts and modern luxuries that society offers, but also think of the generations ahead. I just don't know if it's practical, or even realistic, to think that everybody is going to all of a sudden buy the most fuel efficient car, think very carefully about how they use water, and consider what they can do at home to conserve energy. I don't think it's something that's on everybody's mind, at least not enough to make an impact.

I think it's probably going to take a cataclysmic event for these issues to resonate with people to the extent that they would really be willing to do something. I am not sure that a warmer world, in and of itself, is a particular concern in modernized, industrial societies. People often say, "Well, if it's four degrees warmer, I'll just keep my air conditioner on." I believe that, unfortunately, is the mindset of a typical person. They should also consider the possibility that they will have half as much water available to them. That is something I think will resonate with people. So, yes, I would say that people should be more attuned to the consequences of global warming.

Global warming is still a highly debated issue in our field, with respect to both what we've observed and are predicting. There's still a great deal of uncertainty. That actually is one of the thrusts of this laboratory's research. In our model, we try to address this uncertainty in global climate predictions. Because we have this integrated model, we not only recognize those changes, but also try to understand the consequences of those changes.

The fact that we have an abundant water supply is what makes our world a very unique place. And it's not just that we have water, but that we have water that is constantly and vigorously being recycled. That's the key. How vigorous is that cycle and do we replenish our reservoirs at a rate which is commensurate with depletion?

What role do you see your work playing in a global context? Where do you see it going?

Within my lifetime, or within my career, I would first of all like to see us all arrive at a consensus of what we think is going to happen. I think that is something that is lacking. In some ways, I feel like we're at a paradigm lock. Everybody agrees— from people on my side who study climate hydrology, to people who deal with water resource management– –that a healthy water supply is critically important to us and our planet. We just haven't quite gotten to the point where the information we provide each other spurs action.

Up to now, what generally has happened is that someone will put out a study, or finding, and maybe it finds its way onto the desk of a manager or policymaker who says that it's interesting, but not really what they need. In the NASA project, we operate on the idea that we have to start making our science pay for itself. We've put a lot of funding into basic research and making our global models and predictions better, but there has not been a noticeable return on that investment. The Energy and Water Cycle Study program was actually founded in the applications division, but we have a long-term vision strategy for bona fide benefits. If at the end of my career, I saw that my involvement had made a small difference in the struggle against this global crisis, that would be great.

Do you feel though that the government's policies for industry are enough, or do we need more regulations for energy and water use?

Having worked near Washington DC, I've gained a superficial appreciation for the work of program managers in a science agency like NASA, and all the work they have to do to convince politicians to get behind their programs. I'm not naïve enough to think that we can just simply go down there with a paper or two and demand funding. Politicians have their constituencies to worry about. If you're asking me whether I wish we had more money for research, I absolutely do.

There was a mission headed by a faculty member at the Department of Civil and Environmental Engineering, Dara Entekhabi. He's a close colleague of mine. He was the project scientist for a mission called Hydros. I have to give him a lot of credit. He made it happen. He got it funded and approved. Unfortunately, it was canceled due to budget cuts.

What was it about?

The Hydros mission was an experimental short-term mission to study the latest technology for measuring water storage in the ground. Not only the water storage, but the particular phase of the water storage—whether it was frozen or not frozen. It turns out that the freeze-thaw cycles in the terrestrial systems can play a crucial role, particularly in high latitudes, in the net carbon uptake of the ecosystems. Studies have shown that if you lengthen the growing season in high latitude and boreal regions, you can actually turn a land area from a source of carbon to a sink of carbon. One of the really hot topics is the polar amplification of climate change, and this mission would have resonated on many different fronts. How do the freeze-thaw cycles change? Can we understand how they evolve now? Will that help us predict what the polar amplification effect will be?

Was it canceled on the government level?

Yes, it was canceled on a bureaucratic, government level. NASA had only so much money and they had already approved two other missions. I should add that one of the missions was a carbon observation mission and the other was a mission to monitor the salinity of the ocean—both were very important. It's not that they thought Hydros wasn't important. I'm sure they did. But it underscores my point from before about perception and priorities. The price of the Hydros mission to run its full length, if I have the numbers right, comes close to the cost of launching the Space Shuttle once. I believe one Shuttle mission costs about 250 million dollars. The Hydros mission was budgeted at around the same number. So it makes you wonder if we are really making balanced decisions. Can we exchange one Shuttle mission for a three-year global study of an environmental issue of significant importance? These are tough decisions.

What are the implications of your work? Are there downsides?

The downside of my research is that we are essentially challenged by two things: a limited amount of observational data on our environment and the incomplete detail of computer models. This puts a strain on the fidelity and utility of any model's prediction. It's pretty clear to me that most people are concerned about water issues, and that helps keep me going. But whenever you're talking about weather patterns, you are dealing with uncertainty. We hear weather forecasts every day. Sometimes they get it right, sometimes they get it wrong. It's hard enough to predict the weather five days in advance, much less a hundred years in advance.

The fundamental principles that go into a computer model to predict where a rain event is going to occur are what we call highly parameterized—that is, we don't have a complete picture of how that works, so we have to use relationships that are not based on sound mathematical formulas or fundamental laws. It is one of the key limitations in predicting these changes accurately. If I were to tell somebody it's going to rain x number of times over your area in a hundred years, there's obviously going to be a certain degree of uncertainty. Well, if the degree of uncertainty is so large that the prediction is not useful, then we have a problem. The primary limitation, or downside, to our research is that we are constantly dealing with uncertainty.

Interviewed 4/26/06

JAN WAMPLER

Professor of Architecture

What are you working on here at MIT?

I have several goals I am working toward but I would say the main one is to try to convince MIT that the resources we have here—throughout the entire Institute—could be used to better both the environment and people's lives. Right now, work of that nature is occurring in various departments. Certainly, I'm doing that in my department. But if we could coordinate these efforts, then MIT could be known as a place where the vital issues of the world are being effectively addressed. My concern is that we are too isolated from one another. So what I'm working on, primarily, is trying to involve other departments in the projects I do. I believe you get better solutions by having more people involved from different disciplines.

I think there's something interesting about us architects. We're taught to be individuals, and that's great, but on the other hand, most projects we do are with groups of people. We have to depend on somebody else in order to accomplish something, yet we don't really know how to work together. And I think that might be true of all of MIT. Everyone is off in a corner doing his or her research. We need to learn how to work together. Recently, I gave my students a project for a temporary homeless shelter. They had to work in teams, and while I feared that it might be a disaster, they loved it. It was a great surprise to me. I didn't expect that. They produced good solutions and they worked off of each other. It's a new idea of the artist. The historic notion of the artist is often of someone doing his or her own thing and not caring about anyone else. But that's not really the way it works because, even as artists, we have to talk to each other. So I'd like to investigate ways to help make that happen.

Also, I believe very strongly that we should be teaching people how to be leaders and how to think creatively. It doesn't matter whether they are in architecture or any other field. To know how to do something is important, of course, but we must always think about what we are doing. I think architects are especially guilty of this. We generally take a problem and solve it, but we often don't think about it in its full complexity. That's why we have such ugly, terrible places outside. So, I keep telling my students, "Yes, you have to learn how to draw and build models and design, but more importantly, you have to question everything you are doing. What is the context of a project in relationship to the larger

issues of society and culture? Can you not only see the reflection of society in the work you do, but also look more deeply and see something that society doesn't see?"

I teach not only the architecture studio, but also what I call international workshops. I take students to various countries and expose them to other cultures, other peoples, other languages, and other ways. I think we're becoming increasingly, incredibly, and narrowly Western in our attitude. More importantly, I think the whole world is becoming a monotonous Western place. It doesn't matter where I go, it seems like it could be the same place. Every airport in the world is the same now, with the same shops and the same things. Every city is the same. I find that identities of people throughout the world are being lost, and that's tragic. So I'm trying to teach my students that people are different and that difference is what makes life wonderful. If we were all the same, it would be boring as hell. Of course, in certain fundamental ways we're all similar—we all love, laugh, cry—but it is important to celebrate the subtle differences in whatever way we can. We architects should celebrate through architecture. So I'm teaching my students, through the international workshops, that there are people in Africa who have quite a different attitude than people in Cambridge about what goes on in a day's life, and we're designing for those people. We have the opportunity to open people's minds.

What changes in and around your field in the recent past affect your research today?

I think the field is in a state of chaos right now. There have been great changes in just the last ten years. For instance, digital technology didn't exist, to a great extent, ten years ago. As architects, we don't know what to do with it. We play with it and have a good time, but are we really utilizing it to its potential, or are we just kids playing with a new toy? I think most of the time it's the latter. Nevertheless, this evolution has changed the way we work in the field. Interestingly, in my opinion, digital technology has not yet produced better architecture. I still believe in hands-on experiences. I don't care what is being made or where it takes place, whether it is in the darkroom developing a print or outside building something. It is the idea of making that is important, the hands. In my opinion, the digital world is somewhat removed from this idea. This is something we're struggling with.

Furthermore, in this same time frame, architecture has not had a unified direction. I wish I had been born, for example, during the Bauhaus days when there was an attitude about things that could be shared. It must have been an incredible experience to be in an environment where everybody was working together toward an idea. That must have been beautiful. The so-called modernists, CIAM (International Congress of Modern Architecture) and Team 10, duplicated that to a certain extent, but since that time we have not seen that. We're all out there on our own, so to speak, doing our own individual things. In my field, it's very confusing for students to know what they should do. They see Frank Gehry, and all of a sudden it's, "Ah, this is what we should do." They don't understand that Frank Gehry worked many, many years before getting to that point. And by the way, Gehry is a maker. He worked with his hands. But they don't see that, they see something else. There is a lot of confusion and I think that makes it very difficult to work in this field. What I'm trying to do—again, in terms of what I'm doing here—is to re-examine what is really essential about architecture. To me, that is people, materials, the sun and rain, how to relate to space, how to relate to culture, and how to think about people.

This is another issue, but we live in a lonely crowd. I was at 77 Mass. Avenue the other day and I couldn't believe everybody standing for the light. Absolutely everyone, except me, had an iPod on, plugged in. We were all standing beside each other but there was no communication. iPods are great, you can have a thousand tunes, but this lack of coming together is a serious issue. The changes in technology are scary. These students in the undergraduate class, their whole world—-and mine too, but not to quite the same degree—is about technology, cell phones, their iPods, and the computer. As architects and artists, we have to emphasize the other side. We have to emphasize that people have hands, and hands can do things and make things. There is nothing more rewarding than making something, seeing it, being critical of it, and having other people around you doing the same thing. It doesn't matter what you're making, it's just the art of making—as opposed to just thinking—that is important. That's why I go back to the Bauhaus. If MIT is about the hands and the mind, then the Bauhaus was about that too. The Bauhaus was probably one of the greatest movements in architecture because it did combine both of them. It was one of the great times in history.

Where do you see your work in a global context? Where do you see it going?

It's interesting that because of computers and e-mail, I can do something in Africa and suddenly it's known throughout the world. Therefore, a tremendous amount of information is going around. I get a lot of e-mail from people I don't know who say, "I've heard about your work and I saw it on the Internet. It's interesting. Please send me more information, and, by the way, here's something I'm doing." We're building up a tremendous amount of information and knowledge in a way that has never been possible before. I always say

I can sit here and do something and Berkeley will know about it before I get home. So I think the impact of our work—strangely enough, this is contradicting to what I said earlier––is very strong. It's much stronger than before. I was in Turkey at the International Union of Architects conference and we had what we called the Global Studio. There were a hundred people there and it was amazing to understand what people are doing throughout the world. Now we have a network established and I get ten e-mails a day about it. As a result, there's a tremendous feeling on my part that what I'm doing is having an effect on people around the world. Ten years ago, I don't think I would have ever said that, not because I wasn't doing the work, but because there was no outlet.

As strange as it sounds, I think my work is better known on the international stage than it is at MIT. Now, this goes back to the first issue. In some ways, I'm better known throughout the world than I am here, within other departments and even within my own department. There's an old joke where you go to a conference and you meet somebody from your own school who has the office next to yours, and you find out what they're doing. This is a commentary on our physical environment. At Berkeley, where I've taught in the past, we had a beautiful campus, and you would bump into people, have a cup of coffee, and talk about what you were doing. We don't do that here. There is no place to bump into anybody. You never have the opportunity to expose your work. What's happening at MIT is the world's best-kept secret. There must be incredible things going on in these ugly corridors and we don't have any idea what it is. It's very sad because I think the true breakthroughs are when discussions transcend disciplines. That's where I get my inspiration—not in my discipline, but when I'm talking to somebody else.

What are the implications of your work? Is there a downside?

Is there a downside? Yes. Am I being too romantically idealistic with what I'm trying to teach and what I do, and am I therefore misleading students into thinking they can do more than what is actually possible? I'd like to think not. Am I being too misleading to a community in Zambia when I say, "We're going to build a new health care center," and their hopes and dreams are pinned on it, and then something happens and it doesn't get built? When you take skills and knowledge out into the real world, then you're bringing values to things. The downside is that maybe the world is not going to embrace these values. That's why I don't work in this country, although I would work in New Orleans, maybe. But I've given up on this country as a place where things can happen.

Yet, failure and disappointment are not things to shy away from. I think it's better to give hope and goals and inspiration to people than to be cynical and realistic. I've never been realistic in my life. I've always been a hopeless romantic in the belief that I can do something to help. So I'm countering myself. I said it was a downside, but the upside is that you have to—particularly now, in these unbelievable times that we're living in—foster hope, give encouragement, and try to show another way. This is crucial. Yes, disillusionment is a danger. The world may not be ready for this kind of attitude. Can we do it? I don't know. I can do it in Zambia, and I can do it in Turkey, but can we do it here? I'm not sure. We need a great reformation of values in this country before that can happen, and I'm not talking about Bush's values. But I'm a hopeless optimist and always have always been. I'm going to counteract everything I said. There is no downside. I'm very optimistic.

Interviewed 11/30/05

UTE META BAUER

Associate Professor of Visual Arts
Head of the MIT Visual Arts Program

What are you working on here at MIT?

I work on questions around the production of space in times of instability and flux, and the role of culture and art under such conditions. Last year, I taught a course that focused on art and catastrophes. This year the topic is shelter. We investigate how these terms have been understood historically and we re-evaluate them from a contemporary perspective. What is the potential of input from the arts? DADA is a great historical example, or the Situationists, but there are also many activist practices today. I am interested in what kind of meaning or impulse art can give to people in other disciplines. This type of dialogue and exchange encourages situations where interests overlap and where people from different disciplines work together. Here at MIT, it is widely understood that exchange is necessary. This institution is well known for its problem solving potential. That is the big mandate. I feel that the artists teaching in the Visual Arts Program here at MIT are uniquely suited to make a significant contribution. The complexities of this task are so profound, I believe it is impossible for one single discipline to grasp and handle it all. Additionally, it is very interesting to understand a subject from different points of departure. I very much hope that the arts will become a stronger voice and player within the MIT orchestra.

What kind of artistic practice do you think may best contribute to solutions, or might be interesting in the context you're describing?

One example would be our colleague Krzysztof Wodiczko, who directs the Interrogative Design Workshop. This year he is working on the development of vehicles for war veterans. This vehicle is something that would help the veterans, their families, and those who see the unusual looking device confront first hand the traumatophobia caused by the experience of warfare. Perhaps it will even make people who design other components for the different aspects of warfare a bit more reflective. From a social and commercial aspect, this idea is valuable and overlooked.

What changes in and around your field have affected your work or research?

When I first entered the field, I learned that art is something that should be and can be experienced by everybody, not just by a selected group of people. This is a powerful

notion because it means that not only does art have the potential to stimulate and affect our perception and understanding of the world, but that each of us has access to seeds of this enlightenment. The next step that changed my practice was to realize that there is not necessarily equality within our field. I began looking more into feminism and realized that as a very young director of a German art institution, I was pretty much alone as a woman in such a position. The next step—which I was really able to embrace while working on a big project like Documenta 11—involved understanding inequalities in the contexts of ethnicity and race, and understanding major imbalances in the world in terms of the economical distribution of resources. The arts should have a voice in these issues. Consider somebody like August Sander, who made a generation of workers visible through his photography. That to me is one strong voice. Also Joan Jonas, who works in her performances in a much more symbolic and allegoric form. She communicates profoundly about our world. There is always the possibility and opportunity to make an impact through artistic work. I think often of the work done by NGOs (non-governmental organizations) in areas of crisis. They get involved early and are able to produce rapid changes. Sadly, art and culture always enter much later. In my opinion, that's a big mistake. I believe in cultural involvement. Giving people the tools and forums for individual expression and commentary is crucial, especially in traumatic situations. Having been in the art field for so long, I see a split. You have one side of the market— the commercial side—that grows stronger and stronger, but at the same time disengages more and more from the rest of the world. On the other side, you have those who are actively involved in the cultivation of social awareness and issues of social context. The world though is becoming increasingly and incredibly complex. To remain vital and relevant, art must keep pace with these profound changes. It was very interesting to hear Ole Bauman, a visiting faculty member in architecture, last term. He said, if today everybody is so unique, and has such special projects—which can be distributed through YouTube or MySpace, etc.—maybe the role of art is to free itself from this idea of being unique and, rather, refocus on what it means to be a society or a community. That was a very interesting and challenging idea from him, and it is an opinion I share.

If you look at your work in a global context, where do you see it positioned? Also, where do you see it going in the future?

On one hand, I see myself in a very privileged position and location. I am self-sufficient. I have a job and I can live on my own. That is a privilege. In other parts of the world, it is very difficult, if not impossible, for women or members of lower income classes to gain access to such positions and to enjoy freedom of speech and ideas. On the other hand, I think we can learn a great deal from the rapid development in other parts of the world.

Development has slowed down in the Western Hemisphere, and I am surprised by this stagnation. That makes it exciting for me to collaborate with people in other places and exchange ideas on what it means, or could mean, to be an intellectual.

And the future? You mentioned earlier that you'd like art to be on site faster when things happen.

Being faster on site, but also being better prepared. My goal for the next five years is to actually establish a think tank called CAMP—which stands for Contemporary Art, Media, and Politics—that eventually leads to the founding of a cross-disciplinary center. I think that could be started from within the arts and then integrate other departments and disciplines. I'm not saying that artists should go out and be problem solvers. Instead, I see us contributing to a more general understanding of the problems we all face. Before any problem can be solved, it must first be acknowledged, understood, and discussed in a common language. This millennium has begun violently and it doesn't look like that will end any time soon. Just last weekend, I was in a conference at Cooper Union that dealt with re-negotiating the public sphere and cultural practices. One of the Asian contributors and member of Raqs Media Collective, Shuddhabrata Sengupta, believes that we will soon see large-scale wars in Asia. He said that we are not looking into a future of more peaceful times. We are dealing with significant challenges in the areas of energy, sustainability, and resources. Substantial hard work will be required to maintain peace. We cannot simply assume that is only the job of those who are directly involved with these fields. It is up to all of us to play a role in creating real solutions.

What are the downsides of your work?

Recently I attended a conference at MIT dealing with the level of political engagement of students in universities—where they said that 20 years ago it was a big deal if somebody above the age of 35 entered the room to debate political issues. Today, it's a big deal if somebody below 35 enters the room for such a debate. So, the downside, as I see it, is that due to the huge pressure placed on success and career planning, the ability of the students to see and understand society at large has diminished. The awards of being politically active are not great. Therefore, political awareness has been de-emphasized. There are certainly active movements but, particularly in the U.S., people tend not to engage unless they are affected personally. As educators and researchers, we must not only stress the importance of involvement, but also understand that in today's socio-political landscape the inclination toward activism cannot be assumed. It must be carefully cultivated.

Interviewed 5/7/07

Andrea Frank is an artist and lecturer at the MIT Visual Arts Program in the Department of Architecture. Through a wide range of media, she has addressed subjects such as history, education, memory, and psychology, as well as current issues of global concern. Her work has been exhibited internationally, with recent solo exhibitions at Edward Thorp Gallery in New York and Galleria Michela Rizzo in Venice, Italy.

Frank studied at the Academy of Fine Arts in Munich, Germany, and received her MFA from Parsons in New York. She also participated in the Whitney Independent Study Program. Frank is the recipient of numerous grants and fellowships including the DAAD, Rotary International Foundation, Studienstiftung des Deutschen Volkes and the Council for the Arts at MIT.

For more information please visit http://www.andreafrank.net.